TERRIBLY ENGLISH

A guide for curious natives and baffled visitors

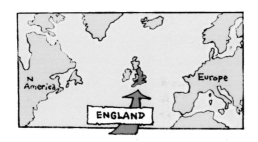

RUPERT BESLEY

Custard, cricket, Shakespeare, fog . . . all that is baffling and impenetrable, all that makes this country what it is (plus several other bits besides) gathered with characteristic modesty and hesitation into the perfect gift for any foreigner. Or native. Er, sort of.

To chris –
Bst wishs !
Bsley

Warning:

Souvenir I

D0227203

ACKNOWLEDGEMENTS

With many thanks to Ernest Hecht and James Doyle of Souvenir Press

Text and illustrations copyright © 2012 by Rupert Besley

First published in Great Britain in 2012 by Souvenir Press Ltd
43 Great Russell Street, London WC1B 3PD

ISBN 9780285640924

Typeset by M Rules

Printed and bound in Great Britain by Bell & Bain Ltd., Glasgow

1. Introduction

England (not to be confused with Britain, GB, G8, UK, K9, Scotland, Ireland, Wales. Or France)

part-time member of the European Union

part of the United Kingdom plus Yorkshire

Location: 21 miles off Cap Gris Nez

Size: roughly 6 times the size of Wales or about the size of Alabama

Capital: London and don't we all know it

Regions: Border, Tyne Tees, Yorkshire, Granada, Central, Anglia, London, Meridian, HTV, West Country

Highest mountain: Scafell Pike, Cumbria, 978m (3209 ft)

Lowest mountain: East Mount, Hull, 11m (36 ft)

[disputed by Holland in Lincolnshire with Pinchbeck Marsh at 8m (25 ft)

Huntingdonshire's high point, Boring Field, clocks in at 80m/263ft]

Imports: footballers, tourists, food, oil, gas, coal, manufactured goods, clothing, rubbish

Exports: Marmite, tribute bands, rubbish

Derivation: England takes its name from the Angles, who were German

Motto: England uses the motto of the British monarchy, *Dieu et mon Droit*, which is French and means 'God and I'm right'.

(Botswana got there first with *Pula*, which means Rain.)

LAKELAND VIEWS

ENGLAND OVERVIEW

England is made up of small villages with names like Boggerthorpe, Scrotely Parvum and Piddling in the Wold. Each nestles cosily in the folds of quilted greenery that is forever England. Each has a Big House, a pond and a green, a small church, a pub, a cricket team, a chinless vicar, a dim constable, a nosy postmistress (but not any more) and, once a week (barring Bank Holidays), a bus out of the place. Tucked away at a respectful distance from the village is a small council estate occupied by howling dogs and difficult locals who throw things at each other.

The Big House is occupied by such members of the gentry as have survived 30 generations of inbreeding, bad food and boarding-school education. Their every need is seen to by a sour-faced butler who knows everything, a kitchenmaid who knows nothing, a rosy-cheeked cook and a gardener with murderous intentions. Once a year the gardens of the Big House are thrown open to the village for the annual extraction of money known as the Summer Fete. Each year, next morning, a body is found in the library. Nothing happens in the countryside. London is where it's at.

London is vibrant, large, multicultural and expensive. London stretches roughly from Margate to Winchester, Bedford to Brighton. London is quite different from the countryside. At its centre is Buckingham Palace, which overlooks Hyde Park and the Serpentine: a Big House, a pond and a green ...

SLEEPY OLD DEVON

TERRIBLY WELCOME

The English have always been sniffy about who they let in to their homes. (You're quite right, that should be 'whom they let into ...' That's another thing about the English: largely incapable of stringing together two words in any other tongue, they fuss terribly over the slightest slip-up of grammar or pronunciation, rushing to correct the person who has abused their precious lingo. Or that's how English people used to behave. Thirty years of educational reform have created a generation no longer able to write or speak in any language.)

The traditional home in England has a front room, for entertaining. This is kept barred and bolted, except for funerals. It's not that the English aren't friendly, just a bit reserved. Or shy. Well, English really.

So, visitors beware. Don't expect to be welcomed in with wet kisses and fond hugs. More of a watery smile, accompanied by observations on the weather. This is followed by detailed questioning over every part of the route taken by you to get this far – a lengthy process, giving your host time to weigh up whether or not you may be suitable for inviting over the doorstep.

It's much the same at ports of entry. Here foreigners are separated out by lanes which lead to small rooms where they are tested on their ability to foxtrot, tell rude jokes or say who won the Boat Race in 1953. Those who fail are taken off to detention centres where they are given time to learn the rules of cricket and develop a liking for custard before being allowed into the Land of the Free.

TERRIBLY POLITICAL

system of government: presidential
political status: infant democracy

Unless forced otherwise by political crisis (eg shock resignation in the Dept of Dog Scoops), the government holds office for a four-year term. England (and Scotland and Wales) invented parliament, fair play, democracy and sunshine. General Elections are held on Thursdays to fit in with television schedules. Every four years there is a secret ballot, on leaving which voters are accosted by two bats with clipboards who will beat the living daylights out of anyone who does not hand over all details.

EXCITEMENT MOUNTS AS ELECTIONEERING KICKS OFF IN THE COTSWOLDS

COUNTIES

England has 39 counties. Or 46. Or 30 ... it depends what you count as county. Are you talking Ceremonial County, Administrative County, Lieutenancy County, Historic County, Registration County, Geographical County, Shire County, Postal County, Police County, Cricket County, Metropolitan County, Non-Metropolitan County, County Palatine or what? For anyone born before 1974, counties are what they've always been: ancient and traditional, coloured yellow, pink, green, blue or orange on the map. These were made up of hundreds, or wapentakes in the North, lathes in Kent and rapes in Sussex. Then along came some bureaucrat, keen to tidy things up and change everything. Out went places like Cumberland, Herefordshire, Rutland, Westmorland and Worcestershire. In came places like Avon, Cleveland and Humberside; but none of them lasted.

Nobody likes being faffed about. Residents of Bournemouth, born and bred in Hants, were not pleased to wake one morning and find themselves in Dorset. Like the bus company that once covered the region, Bournemouth remains an odd combination of Pants and Corset. Folk in the Soke of Peterborough, once part of Northamptonshire, became residents of Huntingdonshire in 1965, only to find that turned into Cambridgeshire nine years later. Lancashire suffered more than most in 1974, losing Widnes and Warrington to Cheshire, Furness to Cumbria, Manchester to itself, made Greater, and Liverpool to Merseyside – but they did manage to snitch a few parts of Yorkshire by way of compensation.

Not that 1974 was the only carve-up of the counties. It's something that has always gone on and will continue, provoking low-level guerilla warfare and the capture of road-signs. Long ago England had Monmouthshire, now in Wales. It also had Bedlingtonshire, Cravenshire, Islandshire, Hallamshire and Norhamshire, though none of them as counties. (Ditto Borsetshire, Mummerset and Wessex.) Meanwhile new places get spawned (Sefton, Sandwell, Thamesdown, Tameside, Thurrock, Knowsley, Halton), only to be abolished by the time anyone has worked out where they are. Then there are the oddities, like Kingdom of Lindsey and Isles of Purbeck, Thanet and Ely. Or places like Tamworth and Newmarket which, till 1888, straddled two counties (Staffs/Warwickshire, Suffolk/Cambs) with a border that ran up the high street. In Todmorden (Yorks/Lancs) it went through the Town Hall. All most trying for any civil servant itching to tinker with boundaries. So change goes on, with large counties (Sussex, Yorkshire) getting hacked into pieces and small ones (Middlesex, Huntingdonshire, Isle of Wight) getting sat on, but refusing to die. All very English: one big muddle.

EARLY INCIDENT ON ENGLAND'S NORTHERN BORDER

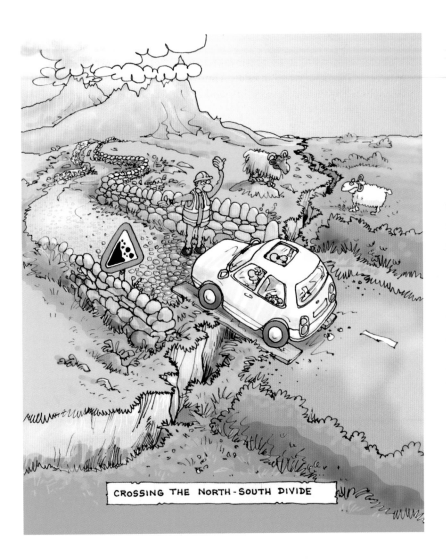

CROSSING THE NORTH-SOUTH DIVIDE

2. Not Terribly

THE TEN COMMANDMENTS IN ENGLISH

1. Thou shalt underplay things generally
2. Thou shalt not leave thy chariot in thy neighbour's parking spot
3. Thou shalt pretend to get the joke even when thou doesn't
4. Thou shalt have a different type of sauce to hide the taste of every dish thou tasteth
5. If thou seeeth a queue, thou shalt join it – at the right end
6. Thou shalt have appalling dress sense
7. Thou shalt mock thy betters
8. Thou shalt spend thy senior years looking out to sea
9. Thou shalt always lose on penalties
10. Thou shalt not talk about things like politics, religion, philosophy, illness, money or sex

ENGLAND PENALTY SHOOT-OUT

BEING ENGLISH

Warm beer, cricket on the green, John Major cycling home from Evensong, moderation in all things – okay, most things, well, some things anyway … Quiet self-deprecation is another virtue much prized by the English, so much so that few even ever admit to being English. Instead they add some let-out clause, like 'Half-Welsh, actually –' or 'Three eighths Scottish on my mother's side'. Bearing in mind that the Anglo-Saxons hailed from Germany and that every wave of settlement and immigration before and since has come from abroad, rabid Anglophiles of the Far Right, waving banners to protect their purity, could be on to something of a loser. The purest English these days are to be found in the plains of Punjab and foothills of Kashmir, whose people still practise perfect manners and RP accents that date from the Raj.

St George, patron saint of England (and Moscow) came from Cappadocia, now Turkey. Or was it Lydda in Palestine? Equally foreign is England's symbolic beast, the lion; big cats here are rare in the wild, except round Bodmin. (The unicorn is Scottish.) Morris dancing (originally 'Moorish') comes from Spain and recent research suggests cricket may have begun on the continent. In fact, a great deal of that which is iconically English has its origins abroad: chips, tea, bungalows, Punch, tikka masala … even the weather has come from elsewhere.

Self-deprecating – me? Not really.

A TRADITIONAL KNEES-UP
TO CELEBRATE SUMMER'S RETURN

The English like to let others know they have the finest police force in the world, the best television, the pleasantest countryside, the greatest pop and the foulest football fans. The English are famous for modesty and understatement.

Inconspicuous abroad and so easily passing off as locals, English people are the ones heard in foreign parts protesting ever louder, 'Onglay! Inglaisy! Inglish ...' until the penny finally drops, allowing the hapless Serb or Catalan on the receiving end to lead off in perfect BBC English. Foreigners can be so dim.

The English do not like to make an exhibition of themselves, which is why they go abroad to do it there instead. They generally prefer not to join in, as with the euro.

STIFF UPPER WOTSIT

It was the death of Diana that did it. When Queen Victoria died, her funeral cortege creaked through the capital in a solemn silence so still that the noise of an early cine-camera was enough to startle a horse in the procession. At Churchill's passing, thousands lined the streets to stare at their feet and sniff in the fog. As the coffin emerged from Kensington Palace on 6 Sept 1997, a low moan went up from the crowd, followed by a wail, and soon all London was awash with tears. In that moment two centuries of pent-up emotion were released and suddenly it was all right to cry. Gazza, too, had a hand in the change, his Wembley tears proving to be a turning-point in English history. Two decades on, everyone does it – footballers, rowers, England cricket captains . . . No sporting event is complete without a good weep and winners are worse than the losers.

The 18th century was the last great era of blubbing. Polite society demanded wet cheeks with much dabbing of the moistening eye. The ultimate accolade for a social gathering was the full swoon, complete with smelling-salts. In all the best drawing-rooms locks were tossed, cheeks ran, chins quivered and waifs enfolded for comforting in copious bosoms; and the women were just as bad.

The needs of Empire put paid to all that. Generations of small boys were sent away from home to be nailed to mantelpieces, toasted on fires, thrashed like corn and trampled into the playing-fields of Eton. From the public schools emerged a new breed of man. Out went cloaks and lace, tights, buckles and wigs (except for judges); in came army wear, toothbrush moustaches and lantern jaws, for clenching on pipes and taking it on the chin. Emotion was kept on a tight rein. Physical contact was rare between the formal handshake of first introduction and the full encounter in marital bed on first night of honeymoon.

My, how things have changed. Post-Diana, time needed for a quick round of the shops has more than trebled to allow for every hug, grope, body-press and tongue-lock expected by all whom you meet. The whole country has gone touchy-feely. Bulldog Drummond would not last two seconds in it.

HUMOUR

Much loved around the world is the famous English Sense of Humour. This consists of laughing at others. Foreigners don't always find this funny, but then they do not have the English Sense of Humour. English comedy goes back a long way. The Anglo-Saxons loved puns. When-is-a-door-not-a-door-when-it's-a-jar (translated into Anglo-Saxon) had them wetting themselves every time. Most cracker jokes date from this period. 'Infamy, infamy – they've all got it in for me!' (Kenneth Williams in *Carry On Up*

The Khyber) is officially England's favourite joke. By Victorian times the SoH had developed into something more subtle and sophisticated, targeting Irishmen, vicars and non-readers of Punch. Often the humour was so subtle it eluded everyone.

By the 1950s England was ready to enter a golden age of humour. Step forward Charlie Drake, Tommy Trinder, Bernard Bresslaw, Brian Rix, Terry & June. Enter Norman Wisdom. Whoops. Then came stand-up and the Satire Boom, followed by Reality TV, opening the floodgates to new forms of mirth. These days, and especially at Christmas, the bookshop shelves groan under the weight of humour of every kind. Willy books, farting books, poo books ... English humour has come of age. This is adult humour.

ECCENTRICITY

Eccentricity is normal in England. The English love oddity; eccentrics are a protected species, unless they move in next to you or sit alongside on the bus.

SHE KNEW IT. SHE JUST KNEW IT.

MANNERS / ETIQUETTE / POLITENESS

Time was when manners mattered. Politeness was pretty well a degree subject in itself, requiring years of careful study. Thick instructional manuals were issued on how to behave at different occasions and in different forms of company – how to address a defrocked archdeacon who is the fifth son of a duke, which table-knife to using when halving a pea and so on. These days nobody gives a toss. Rude is the new polite. Sticks of seaside rock used to carry sweet messages or souvenir placenames; Brighton rock today says things like Tosser, Slapper, Dipstick, Tart. Fat Bastard is one that always sells well. Modern living has swept away the paraphernalia of etiquette and with it all rules of correct and incorrect behaviour. All but one, ignored at your peril: at supermarket checkouts, never fail to place the divider behind your line of purchases or omit to thank the person ahead of you for having done so.

THE MAN WHO FAILED TO PLACE THE DIVIDER
BEHIND HIS SHOPPING AT THE SUPERMARKET CHECKOUT

Modern Manners / as taught in schools

1. When out in town with friends, always walk in line abreast. That pavement's the council's innit, and you've as much right as the next person to be on it, right.
2. When eating, keep your mouth open throughout in order to enable others to share in the gustatory experience.
3. Do not ever say sorry as an apology could be taken as an admission of liability in the event of an insurance claim.
4. In queues, eg at Post Office, keep moving forwards, in close proximity to the person in front. Keep up a regular sniff to encourage movement ahead.

'And this one's for Betty in South America - you remember Betty round the corner who went to Brazil after that business with the window cleaner?'

5. At pavement narrowings, age gives way to youth and both give way to bicycles.

6. Always allow unnecessary wrapping material to fall to the ground. Removal of this provides employment for those less fortunate than yourself. (You can save others some bending by placing drinks cans and fast-food containers in garden walls and hedges.)

7. Have your own signature hoot on the car-horn to deploy down the road at the end of an evening out visiting friends. It'll put a much-needed smile on the face of the neighbourhood.

8. If enjoying a night out and in urgent need of being sick, aim into a front garden rather than on to a well-used pavement.

9. Never give up your seat on a bus or train as such an action could be interpreted as a form of sexual advance.

10. Do not go to the aid of a distressed child as that will certainly be taken as a form of abuse.

11. Quiet carriages are for phone-calls.

12. Motoring: if obliged to wait in traffic, the correct courtesy signal to acknowledge the oncoming driver is a single finger smartly raised, several times.

ORDER OF PRECEDENCE

Take careful note of this when planning a dinner-party or formal occasion –

ETIQUETTE: THE CORRECT PROCEDURE AT DOORWAYS –

Monarch	Baronet
Prince/ss	Dog
Duke/Duchess	Knight
Footballer	Person
Marquess/Marchioness	Cat
Earl/Viscount	Non-entity
Model	Criminal
Archbishop	Slime Mould
Pop Star	Estate Agent
Baron	Banker
Celeb	Planner

NATIONAL COSTUME

The national costume of England is a blue anorak over beige cardy with gardening trousers. It is worn on Sundays, holidays and special occasions. Dressing for dinner is still normal in England, except in nude barbecue circles. Attending formal dinners and social functions is a business so fraught with sartorial hazard that many people choose to stay home instead.

Scotland has kilts, the Welsh have pointy hats, but the English have only school uniform to fall back on. It's an old habit that dies hard. Englishmen order their wardrobes along the lines of clothing-lists from long ago, which explains the dubious items of games kit that come out on summer holidays. For updating regulations, there is a Cabinet Committee that meets twice yearly in secret to hammer out issues of dress code; their findings are conveyed to buyers at Marks & Spencer and signalled to the public by BBC presenters of news and weather. Currently, for men, the uniform for smart-but-not-formal is blue shirt with yellow tie.

The English do not do fashion as do Italians or chic Parisians. They feel no need to don fine feathers for the world outside. So they do drab and dowdy instead. The higher you are in society the more likely you are to dress as the dog's breakfast. Pinstripe suits and waistcoats are for trainee managers in chainstores; ballgowns and tails are for plumbers and parking-attendants out on the dance-floor. The aristocracy prefer to be seen in tweeds well chewed by labrador and barbours spattered with badger-puke, vole-snot and pâté. The professional, paper-pushing middle classes have shirt and tie and, unless wishing to give outrage, this means white shirt and dark tie with small crests or sober diagonal line. Women at work have the choice between appearing as billowing milkmaids or cutting a mean figure in angular power suit. Working-class folk are allowed sportswear and designer labels in the form of t-shirts, polo-shirts, shorts, leggings and trainers, with shell-suits for formal occasions.

NATIONAL COSTUME:

SCOTLAND   ENGLAND   WALES

Despite the apparently casual attitude to codes of dress, the English do retain certain rules and close watch is kept by CCTV in ports and town-centres to see these are observed. Common errors include:

- the tucking of shirt into underpants
- the allowing of tie to hang out over jumper
- the accompanying of dark suit with brown shoes
- the wearing of black bow tie with lumberjack shirt
- the doing up of bottom button of the waistcoat

NATIONAL EMBLEMS

The flag of England (obligatory on white vans, though no longer so on ambulances) is the Cross of St George. This was pinched from Genoa around 1190.

1st draft of heraldic design
for the Coat of Arms for England

The national coat of arms shows Three Lions stretching and scratching. Lions do not normally grow in England. The Tudor rose is the floral emblem of England. This is a rose with a white centre and red outer petals. That was the device chosen by spinne-doctors at the York-Lancaster marriage which ended the Wars of the Roses, once they had decided not to go for pink.

NOT THE NATIONAL ANTHEM

God save our gracious Queen,
Long live our noble Queen,
La la la la.
Thingy um victorious
Happy er glorious
La la la la-la la,
God save the Queen.

These words, sung by footballers on great occasions, are not the national anthem of England. Nor is *Jerusalem*, much sung by Women's Institutes. Nor, yet, are the following:

- *Land of Hope and Glory*
- *Swing Low, Sweet Chariot*
- *The Birdie Song*
- *Come on, Rooney*

England does not have a national anthem. Official. (It uses the national anthem of the UK instead.)

♪ Bring me my arrows of desire ♪

3. Terribly House & Garden

The French can pass a whole night sat round a table discussing whether or not the table exists. Germans rarely turn down the chance of a nice dip into Herder or Kant. But the English can't be fussed with philosophy – all too airy-fairy and highbrow for a nation that prides itself on its pragmatism. The English are down-to-earth, practical folk, good with their hands if poor with their brains. That's why German windows open in all directions, for easy cleaning, while English systems require telescopic devices available by mail order, ladders, scaffolding, cradles etc in order to wipe the other side of the glass. And that's why French utilities run together in common ducts with easy access to the side of the road, while the English have to close the highway and throw up an open-cast mine every time there's a problem with the gas, water, electricity, cable TV, drains you name it. And it's why the French have the wit to use the same numbers for department/postcode/car no/phone no, while the

English go for different combinations every time. No, the English aren't remotely practical. 'Practical' means acceptance of standardisation and systematic thinking, but that kind of thing smacks far too much of jackboot on the neck for English thinking. No one in England wants to be made to do the same as everyone else. What Brighton does, Hove does differently. Why else did they fight two world wars? Nobody's going to tell the English what colour to paint their front-door, when to take school holidays, whether it's pints or litres. Red tape, petty bureaucracy, health and safety, political correctness gone mad. It's all there in Magna Carta, you go and see. Individual liberties matter in England, more than most things, including pragmatism.

AN ENGLISHMAN'S HOME IS HIS SHED

Blame Samuel Smiles, with his self-help books, or Baden-Powell maybe, with his readiness to solve all the world's problems with a clove hitch, a clean handkerchief and two bits of string. Do-It-Yourself is a national affliction. Christmas is a time for giving socket-sets. The adjustable spanner was invented by an Englishman; to this day 'Englander' in German can mean either Englishman or adjustable spanner, depending on circumstances. (Those war-comic Nazi pilots screaming 'Englander!' from smoke-filled stricken aircraft may not have been so stupid after all.)

The one thing every deskbound Englishman dreams of is retirement, with the prospect of finding a little place close to the sea and in need of attention. Come the big day, alongside the Twiglets trolley and cheesy speeches, he will be presented with workmate, power drill and wrecking equipment. Then, with steely determination never to have to pay again for professional services, he will set to work on his newly acquired bungalow, destroying everything in it. Exeunt by skipload ornamental features and structural necessities that once had craftsmen whistling in pride at their handiwork; enter the world of dodgy DIY ... Twenty years pass, walls crack, ceilings bulge, mould can't believe its luck. A single explosion rocks the neighbourhood and the unfortunate Oddjob is transferred to Casualty with lengths of gas piping plumbed into his rear. Time for another pair, newly retired, to view the property, suck hard on their teeth and announce, 'We'll soon have this place back on its feet'.

GARDEN

Where'er the summer air doth waft,
Twixt mansion, hall or homely croft,
Tis there sweet perfume of the rose
Doth carry and get up your nose . . . .
from *England's Bower* by Prudence Long.

The traditional cottage garden is something cultivated by the English and coveted by the French. It is a riot of pastel colour, where bees hum on busy flight-paths between lupin, hollyhock, delphinium and rose. Such gardens do not exist, except in jigsaws. Mostly they have been grubbed out to make way for patterns of brick and concrete for off-road parking and floods in Tewkesbury. Rear-gardens have stripy lawns, productive veg gardens and nosy neighbours. Real gardens have slugs, aphids, dustbins, feral cats and washing.

There is a basic division between those who like to work their garden and those who don't. Those who do, have different ways of going about it, be that gnomes and paint, chippings and gravel or strimmer, chainsaw, flame-thrower and toxic spray to nuke the place free of pest and weed. The garden is a place of rest.

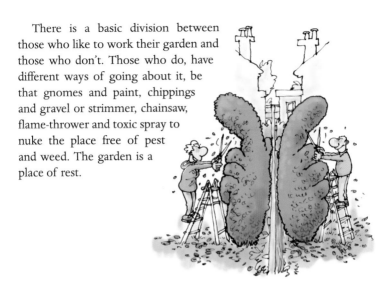

TERRIBLY DOGGY

Dog ownership is not compulsory in England, but it is expected. Have no dog and it will be assumed that instead you have a cat. Choice of dog is important. Many people go just for matching hair colour or teeth, which can be a mistake. In settling on a make of dog, it is worth paying attention to the info on origin and default mode that is carried in the brand name. Thus, Yorkshire terriers come from Yorkshire; labradors from Labrador, lapdogs from Lapland, mongrels Mongolia. Retrievers retrieve, pointers point and springers knock your teeth out.

All dogs in time come to resemble their owners, spending their days slumped across the furniture, with occasional forays into the garden or down the road and back to relieve their flatulence. Some dog-owners take a real interest in their appearance. Local, regional and national shows enable breeders to get together and have the chance to win prizes for poise and gait, condition, obedience and teeth. Months of preparation go into those special moments when owners must lollop round the ring to show off their canines and hope to catch the judge's eye.

Dog ownership, particularly among urban-dwellers, is a throwback to the days when everyone lived on the land, surrounded by animals and chin-deep in excrement. Some forms of ownership hark back to older times, when it really was necessary to have a 3-headed monster with halitosis and fangs to guard the entrance to the cave. 'It's all right, he's only being friendly –' you'd hear from the depths, as the beast out front was busy flailing your limp body against the rocks to crush the bones for ease of pas- sage through its digestive system.

DOG TRAINING

Training classes are available in all areas. Encouraged by frequent pats, promises of a biscuit and the occasional sharp tug on the choke chain, dog-owners soon acquire the rudiments of obedience. Doggy deposits are a source of endless fascination to small children who love to slide. Local authorities these days have bins in dog-walking places, though getting your pet to perform into the receptacle from any distance can test the patience of even the most dedicated owner.

Well-known English Dog Breeds:

Churchill, Andrex, Dulux (used in the manufacture of paintbrushes), Yorkshire, Cerberus, Yapalot, Grottweiler, Staffordshire Bull.

DOG·BREEDS OF EAST ANGLIA

4. Terribly Gastro

Eating out used to be a rarity in England but is these days increasingly popular. At the same time home cooking has got a whole lot more adventurous under the gentle encouragement of several generations of TV chef.

EATING OUT

The core elements of English cookery are custard and gravy. A well-appointed gravy is thick with regular lumps. These contain all the goodness. Allowed to rest, the gravy should form a protective grey skin, which holds in the flavour. Custard is quite different, being yellow. A poor custard or gravy is thin and splattery, with surface bubbles.

Served on its own, gravy may make an appetising soup or starter (chilled). Thickened and containing one carrot and one potato, gravy becomes a favourite dish of the 1950s, mince and two veg. Drizzled over bone and gristle of beef, pork or creature we don't ask after, gravy is central to the famous English Sunday Roast. In its concentrated form, gravy is bottled as brown sauce, spread in sandwiches, smeared on toast or sipped from hot mugs by invalids. Gravy is still made in large factories in the Midlands and distributed by tanker. It is the mainstay of English cooking.

Vegetables, such as sprouts and cabbage, are traditionally boiled for 40 mins or until the kitchen is filled with steam and smelling of volcanoes. Root vegetables may take a little longer, especially for that fashionable chargrilled flavour achieved by allowing the pan to boil dry.

For Marcel Proust the taste of a petite madeleine dunked in tea was enough to unlock the memories of childhood. For English readers of a certain age, a brief roll-call of standard school dinners will do much the same:

- Horsemeat, cabbage & mash; frogspawn & jam
- Liver & onion with swede; Baby's Bottom
- Spam fritter, carrots & mash; Dead Man's Leg
- Worms with bullets; Fly Cemetery
- Dog Stew, butterbeans & mash; prunes
- Mince with maggots & peas; prunes again
- Brains in cheese; stodge with Cat Sick
- Smoked haddock with eyeballs; bread & butter pudding
- Leftovers

There weren't overweight children in those days.

RECIPE CORNER

Simple Suggestions for Every Class

1 Nibbles (Upper)

Get cook to knock up some savoury thingies to go with drinki-poos. We've got the Wriothesley-Turbotts dropping in this evening, along with the Household Cavalry.

2 Cucumber Sandwiches (Middle)

Take one thin-sliced loaf, lightly butter and remove crust from all sides of each slice. Top, tail and remove skin of cucumber. Cut into slices thin enough to be able to read Daily Telegraph through each. Arrange between two pieces of bread, season and cut into isosceles triangles. Arrange on plate in interlocking circles; garnish on top with 5 lengths of cress, decoratively placed. Serve with choice of teas to vicars on deckchairs to plink-plonk of tennis party.

3 Bacon Sarnie (Working)

Get pan of fat on fast burn, add generous rashers and have fire-blanket alongside. Remove bacon from pan once visibility in kitchen is down to two feet. Place between well-buttered slices of thickly cut bread. Squirt with ketchup, relish, grease-gun and mayo. Enjoy.

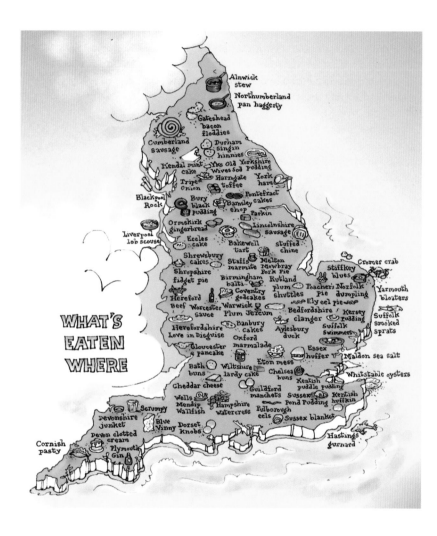

WHAT'S EATEN WHERE

Alnwick stew
Northumberland pan haggerty
Gateshead bacon floddies
Cumberland sausage
Durham singin hinnies
Kendal mint cake
Ye Old Yorkshire Wives Sod Pudding
Harrogate toffee
York ham
Tripe Onion
Blackpool Rock
Bury black pudding
Pontefract cakes
Barnsley chop
Parkin
Ormskirk gingerbread
Lincolnshire sausage
Liverpool lob scouse
Eccles cake
Bakewell tart
stuffed chine
Shrewsbury cakes
Staffs marmite
Melton Mowbray Pork Pie
Stiffkey blues
Cromer crab
Shropshire fidget pie
Birmingham balti
Rutland plum
Poacher's Pie
Norfolk dumpling
Yarmouth bloaters
Coventry godcakes
Ely eel pie
Hereford Beef
Worcester Sauce
Warwick
Plum Jercum
Bedfordshire clanger
Kersey pudding
Suffolk smoked sprats
Herefordshire Love in Disguise
Banbury cakes
Oxford marmalade
Aylesbury duck
Suffolk Swimmers
Gloucester pancake
Essex huffer
Maldon sea salt
Eton mess
Bath buns
Wiltshire lardy cake
Chelsea buns
Whitstable oysters
Cheddar cheese
Guildford manchets
Kentish puddle pudding
Sussex
Kentish huffkin
Wells
Mendip Wallfish
Hampshire watercress
Pulborough eels
Pond Pudding
Scrumpy
Blue Vinny
Dorset Knobs
Sussex blanket
Devonshire junket
Devon clotted cream
Plymouth Gin
Cornish pasty
Hastings gurnard

32

Pasty

Cornish pasties began as portable lunches for tin-miners. In cold winters wives could deliver these warm to the workplace. A genuine Cornish pasty or hoggan therefore has pastry casing tough enough to withstand being dropped down a mineshaft.

Testing pasties at a
Cornish tin mine

Pastymakers fall into two camps, top-crimpers and side-crimpers, and much is argued over the superiority of each. A giant pasty, six foot long, is made each year for the Regatta Week in Fowey and enjoyed by the locals, but for the end bit. The humble pasty makes a surprise appearance in Ancient Rome in Shakespeare's *Titus Andronicus*. The play ends with Titus baking Chiron & Demetrius in a large pie served to their mother –

> *Hark, villains! I will grind your bones to dust,*
> *And with your blood and it I'll make a paste;*
> *And of the paste a coffin I will rear,*
> *And make two pasties of your shameful heads:*

WEST COUNTRY AILMENT:
PASTY CRIMPER'S FINGER

No word there, though, as to the direction of the crimping.

Cornwall is famous also for its pies. Chief of these is Star Gazey Pie – that's the one with pilchards, sardines or small herring (depending on the day's catch) poking heads out through the pastry. Then there's Muggety Pie (made with sheep guts, parsley, cream, pepper and salt), Squab Pie, Likkey Pie, Tetty Pie, Conger Tiddago Pie, Nattlin Pie and Bottom Pie.

Skipper's not
been having
much joy
in the boat –

Conger Pie

Bottom Pie

Other traditional Cornish treats

gurts	–	porridge
crevan	–	hard dry crust
kittle-brath	–	drink made from pouring boiling water on hard dry crust
tow-rag	–	dried codfish
baggly-ow	–	also dried codfish
scoggan	–	boiled mackerel head
fuggan	–	pastry cake
hoggan	–	inferior pasty; unleavened dough with green pork embedded
suchy-meat	–	pudding made of small entrails

Sussex Pudding

Sussex author the Revd W Parish had this to say of Sussex Pudding in 1875 –

Sussex Pudding. A compound of flour and water made up in an oblong shape and boiled. There is a moment, when it is first taken out of the saucepan, when it can be eaten with impunity; but it is usually eaten cold and in that form I believe that it becomes the foundation of all the ills that the Sussex spirit and flesh are heir to. It promotes a dyspeptic form of dissent which is unknown elsewhere. It aggravates every natural infirmity of temper by the promotion of chronic indigestion, and finally undermines the constitution.

Another name for Sussex Pudding is Hard Dick.

The Full English Breakfast is something eaten only by foreigners in dodgy B & Bs and those with hangovers at Sunday lunchtime. It consists of everything in the freezer, plus a few things the cat brought in, hard-fried on to a plate. Full consumption is a test of virility that few like to fail. The FEB removes the need for further intake into the digestive system for several days. However, subsequent travels should be planned round the provision of comfort-stop facilities (latnav advised).

FOOD OF THE GODS

Gobstoppers, humbugs, bootlaces, chews ... we all nurse fond memories of the food we grew up on. Here's a few more to bring a lump to the throat:

biscuits

rich tea, lincoln, suggestive, wafer, ginger nut, bourbon, toothbreaker, squashed flies, custard cream, those ones with the blob of fake jam in the middle, iced gem, malted milk

SPRINGTIME ON A CORNISH PASTY FARM

DRINKS

The preferred drink of the English is something warm and wet, brown and sweet, lightly decorated with a small head of surface scum and tasting of nothing in particular. If it comes in a cup, it's tea; in a mug, it's coffee; in a glass, it's beer. The English are famously drinkers of tea. This can be made from coffee powder. In canteens and tea-rooms, coffee and tea come from the same urn, but are served in different shaped pots. Modern technology goes one better than this with machines capable of dispensing, into paper cup or floor area of your choice, at the press of a button an instant hot drink: soup with milk and two sugars, topped Italian-style with a sprinkling of chocolate. Once you have acquired a

'You will turn into an old bag —'

taste for the above, you will be ready to move on to exploring the full range of brown drinks in England: ovaltine, horlicks, brown ale, bovril, mead, cocoa, cough mixture, own brand cola, English sherry, dandelion and burdock . . .

PARTY TIME

Of all the occasions for a knees-up, that most English of gatherings is the Cheesy Wine Party, 6-8 pm, RSVP. This will be a stand-up do, in smart-cas, which members of the golf-club and selected neighbours will be carded to attend and demonstrate their knowledge of house-prices plus sleight-of-hand with glasses of warm wine and assorted nibbles. Enter the packed living-room with arms folded upward and hands by chin: that way you should manage in the press to get a drink to your lips, while avoiding the menace of a damp handshake. Stick to the dead mice on Ritz biscuits; if tempted by anything on a cocktail-stick, be it cat-turd or pineapple chunk with cube of coloured cheddar, seek out a suitable cushion or portion of sofa in which to secrete the stick. Beware of vol-au-vents, the grey filling of which can seal off windpipe and gullet, leaving the victim to turn purple, while giving out a lava-shoot of flaky pastry to rain down into each drink. After two hours all present will have stepped back on to every other attendee, the party will have been deemed a success and guests will be free to stumble out to odd vehicles and wake next day with blinding headache in an unfamiliar bed.

5. Merrie England
(does not include Yorkshire)

Friday night,
Friday night,
We all get tight
On Friday night.

This beer's flat –
Mine's all cloudy –
There's a terrible draught by this door –

WHINGE DRINKERS

Friday night is traditionally the time to go out on the town, though riots can be spread to extend over a whole weekend or more.

CHRISTMAS

Christmas lasts from September to January 6th. It is considered unlucky still to have decorations up after this date and smug to have done all the shopping before the end of August. Late summer is the time for plans to be laid for who goes where for the festive season. Christmas is a time for all the family to fall out.

I see you've done your decorations –

The ways in which the English choose to mark the holy birth divide along class lines. On council estates competitions are held to see who can use up most electricity with Winter Wonderland decorations in the worst taste. The middle classes celebrate the event by sending out newsletters listing all their children's many achievements, balanced with sombre footnotes detailing the writer's ailments over the preceding year. The upper classes escape to Klosters.

THE FESTIVE YEAR
dates may vary

1 Jan	Burning the Bush at Putley Water Mill, Herefordshire: a bush stuffed with straw is thrown on to a fire
	Wheelbarrow Race, Ponteland, Newcastle (dating back to 14th cent)
	Apple Howling, Henfield, Sussex (howling at apple trees to wake them up)
	New Year's Day swims, Shanklin, Whitley Bay, Whitehaven, Broadstairs . . .
6 Jan	Haxey Hood Game (700 yr old village combat involving 4 pubs, 1 Fool, 11 boggins: early precursor of Rugby League). Wassailing. Molly Dancing.
7 Jan	Candle Auction, Hubberholme.
11 Jan	Whittlesea Straw Bear procession.
3 Feb	Blessing the Throats, St Ethelreda's Church, London
20 Feb	Olney Pancake Race (1st prize: a kiss from the verger, 2nd prize: two . . .)
	Shrove Tuesday football at Ashbourne, Derbyshire, played over two days by Two teams of several thousand players with goals three miles apart. Main rules: murder is prohibited and the ball may not be hidden in a rucksack or carried in a motorised vehicle
	Scarborough Skipping Day: Shrove Tuesday, long-rope skipping on the Promenade in Scarborough
5 Mar	St Piran's Day, Cornwall, march across the dunes, plays and re-enactments
18 Mar	World Poohsticks Championship, Dorchester, Oxon (recent winning teams and individuals have come from Australia, Japan & the Czech Republic)

THE PIRAN VOYAGE

Ill-fated attempt to re-enact the epic journey of St Piran,
who sailed from Ireland to Cornwall on a millstone (or who,
in another version of the tale, was rolled off a cliff while tied to a millstone
on which he miraculously floated back to land at Perranzabuloe).

6 Apr	Easter bun added to the collection at Widow's Son pub, Bromley-by-Bow
9 Apr	Bottle kicking and hare pie, Hallaton, Leics ('The rules are very simple; there aren't any,' according to the Chairman of the trad Easter village brawl). Bacup Nutters' Dance, Lancs.
	World coal carrying championships, Gawthorpe, Yorks
17 Apr	Tutti Men of Hungerford, clutching their poles, collect kisses from the ladies
27 Apr	World Dock Pudding Championship, Hebden Bridge (culinary stardom for common weed)
1 May	Padstow Obby Oss. Otley maypole (celebrating 300 years of pagan revels in local car-park); Bolster Day, Chapel Porth, Cornwall: re-enactment of true story of the giant Bolster (who ate children and people at random, and made Mrs Bolster carry rocks on her back all day) and how local girl Agnes got the better of him
6 May	Wormcharming championship, Blackawton, Devon
May	Pot Walloping Festival, Westward Ho!
8 May	Helston Flora Day and Furry Dance

12 May	Eurovision Song Contest
	Randwick Wap, Glos: Mop Man leads procession through village to dunk mayor in pond
	Public weighing of mayor and dignitaries, High Wycombe
28 May	Cheese rolling, Coopers Hill, Stroud. Woolsack races, Gumstool Hill, Tetbury

ARTISTIC ST IVES

1 Jun	Shin-kicking at Cotswold Olimpicks
4 Jun	Yorkshire Pudding Boat Race, Brawby, N Yorks
16 Jun	Stinging Nettle Eating championship, Marshwood, Dorset (76ft of nettles in one hour is the current record)
19 Jun	Ladies Day, Ascot: a stunning display of hats in the enclosure beforehand and an extraordinary sight as they stream up the final furlong
21 Jun	30,000 gather in the rain at Stonehenge to see the sun not rise over the ancient stones
22 Jun	Filly Loo dance, Ashmore, Dorset
29 Jun	World Worm Charming Championship, Willaston, Cheshire

14 Jul	Pea Shooting championship, Witcham, Cambs
15 Jul	British Pedal-Car Grand Prix, New Milton, Hants
19 Jul	Hot Pennies Day, Honiton
21 Jul	World Championship Snail Racing, Congham, Norfolk
Jul	Crop Circle quests, Wiltshire

2 Aug	Pasty Day, Morvah, Cornwall
12 Aug	Mobile phone throwing championship, Twickenham
25 Aug	Burning the Bartle, Wensleydale: effigy is stabbed and burnt
Aug	Birdman of Bognor contest. Also at Worthing – dates vary.

8 Sept	Canine freestyle dancing competition, Markfield, Leics
10 Sept	Abbots Bromley Horn Dance; Onion Eating Competition, Newent, Glos
11 Sept	Black Pudding Throwing Championship, Ramsbottom, Lancs
12 Sept	Newent Onion Eating competition, Forest of Dean
15 Sept	Gurning Contest, Egremont, Cumbria

2 Oct	Old Man's Day, Braughing, Hants: ceremonial sweeping of leaves from path also Mangold Hurling Championships, Sherston, Wilts
8 Oct	World Conker Championships, Ashton, Northants
31 Oct	Punky Night, Hinton St George, Somerset: children parade by candle-lit mangel-wurzels

5 Nov	Pixxie Day, Shebbear, Devon: large boulder turned over
5 Nov	Ottery St Mary people run through streets with burning barrels of tar on their backs ...
17 Nov	World's Biggest Liar Contest, Cumbria (lawyers & politicians barred from entering)

| 31 Dec | ... they do the same in Allendale, Northumberland Maldon Mud Race |

Who says the English don't know how to enjoy themselves?

ENGERLUND SWINGS LIKE A PENDULUM DO

FLOWER POWER (40 years on)

... bobbies on bicycles two by two. Well, maybe it did once, but that was in the Sixties, when anything was possible. Carnaby Street. Love. Peace. Herman's Hermits. I'm backing Britain. On now to the next generation of rebellious movers and shakers, with their spiky haircuts, sharp suits and eyes set firmly on investment portfolios. Only they, too, have now had their day.

TEN THINGS TO DO IN ENGLAND
BEFORE YOU DIE

1   stare at Buckingham Palace and wonder what's happening
2   empty your wallet on tea at the Savoy (or Ritz or Dorchester or ...)
3   watch England lose at football/cricket/rugby/conkers
4   take a punt on the Cam (it was the undoing of the Revd Spooner, visiting from Oxford)
5   eat a whole candy floss and not throw up in the dodgems
6   stand on the very spot where Shakespeare may have stood (or possibly Bacon)
7   attend a local council meeting and not lose the will to live
8   lose money on a horse with three legs and long teeth
9   drink flat warm beer and claim it's good
10 get a lump in the throat at that first glimpse of the greyish cliffs of Dover

PASTIMES

Morris Dancing

There are two things required of a Morris Dancer of either gender: rhythmic knees and a beard. Before signing on with any side, newcomers should get acquainted with the colourful history of Morris and understand the differences between, say, the Morris Ring and the WMF; Open Morris and Back Street Morris; Official Morris, Extreme Morris, Fullblown, Cotswold, Border, Mixed Sex, Hardcore, Morries (the Provisional Wing of the organisation) and so on. Disagreements between factions have led to ugly encounters with high-stepping knees in groins the main cause of injury.

TERRIBLY SPORTING

England's sporting heroes fall into two camps, gentlemen and players. Gentlemen bring class and breeding to their chosen sport. Immaculate in white, they do not sob or swear and rarely sweat. Gentlemen come from the Home Counties and have been to public school, where they have learnt to lose – like gentlemen. They have broad shoulders, on which they carry the hopes of the nation, and a firm chin on which to take defeat. Gentlemen come second, but do so in heroic style. Come on, Tim.

Players do things differently – think Gazza, Flintoff or Rooney. Players come from the north and have stout necks and fiery tempers. Players win and when they do, you know about it.

It's not just the participants that divide on class lines; the sports themselves are similarly split. Dressage and real tennis are distinctly upper; likewise rowing and polo. Dogs and darts are less so. Rugby union is for one lot, rugby league the other. Horse-racing, the sport of kings (and queen-mothers), does its best to appeal to all levels, but the allocation of duties is not entirely even. Owners, wearing top-hats, crowns or feathered roadkill ('fascinators'), get to pocket the prizes. The lower orders have the job of sitting on the horse or cleaning out the stable. Racegoers are separated by class into different enclosures for the avoidance of cross-pollination.

FIRST STEPS IN HORSEMANSHIP

CRICKET

In 2002 Didier Marchois, former President of France's Cricket Federation, set teacups rocking across the south of England by claiming the game was invented by the French. Citing medieval documents that spoke of matches round Crecy and Agincourt, Marchois stated, 'They leave no room for doubt. Cricket was born in the north of France and taken across the Channel by English soldiers who picked it up from us during truce periods in the Hundred Years War.' As accepted history, the French claim met with little success, but as a Cross-Channel wind-up, it was better than most. French cricket is a game not among the top sports in England.

Everyone knows that cricket was invented by shepherds on the South Downs and in the Wealds of Kent and Sussex. What else was there to do all day but chuck things at twigs balanced on wicket gates – or defend the twigs by batting missiles clear with a length of willow? Sheep were trained to take catches in the outfield (the whites worn by cricketers hark back to those days). And shepherds' wives made the tea. Cricket is all about tea. The object of the game is to be first ones back into the pavilion at four, leaving the opposition to follow on at the sponge cake and sandwiches. To achieve this requires complicated manoeuvres on the pitch and in the outfield, as well as calculations of over rate, asking rate, tea-urn readiness and when to declare.

Cricket has many rules, almost the first of which was introduced at Hambledon in 1741 after one 'Shock' White of Ryegate came to the wicket with a bat that was wider than the set of stumps behind him. Thereafter, bats were limited to a maximum breadth of just over four inches. Cheating or playing a fast one is not cricket, not unless your name is WG Grace (or Hubert Jardine, should you be from Down Under).

Colour television has changed the modern game of cricket almost beyond recognition, but traditional forms of the sport survive in the wild. It is a game of attrition, in which one side sets out to end the other's will to live. It requires a large cricket ground, 22 players, 2 umpires, 4 tea ladies and 6 spectators. One match can go on for several days and even nights, in which case the two batsmen ('nightwatchmen') have to stay at the crease through hours of darkness to guard against a fall of wicket. The game is begun by the bowler (in bowler hat), who must hurl the ball at the vulnerable parts of the batsman, until the latter declares he can take no more and calls for tea. A batsman may be bowled out, caught out, run out, stumped or simply booed off the pitch. When the bowler has bowled an over, he hands over to another bowler. If the bowler goes over his line before bowling, the ball he bowls will be a no ball and the batsperson will still be in, even if he/she is out.

Followers of the game should be familiar with the following terms:

rabbit, long hop, duck, donkey drop, quack trick, spider graph, pie thrower, crumble, jaffa, anchor, beamer, seamer, chinaman, yorker, leg bye, goodbye, googly, pongo, gully, goolies, box, square leg, silly point, off, **** off, backward short leg, stupid leg, have England gone and lost again?

England is home to sport of many kinds. A disproportionately large number of the sports and games played round the world today were invented or first organised and regulated by the English: not judo, of course, basketball or baseball, but soccer, rugby, tennis, cricket – even downhill skiing, which is quite something for a country short on mountains and snow.

Inventing a game does not have to mean being good at it. Indeed, the more England gets hammered at its own prize sport, the more it is inclined to change the rules or slink back to the drawing-board in search of something different. All around the country new forms of competition are being developed and old sports re-invented: dwile-flonking, euchre, rings, worm-charming, welly-throwing, lawnmower racing (British Association series through Sept-Oct), apple-bobbing, snail-racing, grower of the straightest bean, rudest carrot etc. None of these yet has got anywhere near Olympic status or even made it on to Saturday afternoon television, but give them time. Rugby must once have looked equally silly, and cricket still does.

'ANYONE FOR TENNYSON?'

6. Terribly Cultured

ART

Holbein, Hals, Rubens, Van Dyck, Tretchikoff ... many of England's greatest painters have one thing in common: they weren't English. The English have always had their suspicions of the arty-farty, preferring to leave that kind of thing to foreigners, especially if the result is all garlands and cherubs. The English don't know much about art, but they know what they like – usually something brownish and restrained, with a quadruped in it. To English eyes, the only good art is scenery, ideally with horse or dog. Landseer had it all and is up there with Thelwell as England's favourite artist.

Many of the nation's treasures are held in the National Gallery, from Richard II (stags) to Gainsborough's Mr & Mrs Andrews & dog Spot, from Constable's Haywain (horse) and the works of Stubbs (more horses) to Turner's famous Rain, Steam, Speed and Hare. All great art in England has to have a good animal in it – a point not lost on Damien Hirst.

After landscape, the only other thing to appeal to the English is a fine seascape, preferably one with a bit of narrative action (death of Nelson sort of thing). Or a sunset. Cue Turner. Probably the top-selling print of all time is that one with waves that turn into white horses which they used to sell in Boots.

The perfect picture for an English wall would show a lively sea bucking against the low sun in a pink sky. In the middle-ground would be a traditional sailing-barge with drunken captain asleep at the helm; behind the boat, in a circle of ripples, would be the drowning form of a horse gone overboard. At the centre of the composition would be a brave spaniel, about to sink its teeth into the helmsman's crotch in order to raise the alarm. It would probably be called something like Resolution, or The Biting Temeraire, and would go well on place-mats and tea towels. Bung a bit of glitter on the wave-crests and it might even do as a Christmas card.

1st draft (saved from the bin):
HOLBEIN'S HENRY VIII

ARCHITECTURE

The English don't do great architecture. That's the kind of inflammatory statement that will set off any anglophile buildings buff. It fails to recognise the soaring cathedral splendours of Norwich and Salisbury, Ely and Wells, the grandeurs of an Oxbridge college or a Hampton Court, the genius of a Hawksmoor or Wren. But, as with all ignorant half-truths, it does have a point. Go looking for architecture in England and much of what you find is stuff nicked from Italy, France and Ancient Greece.

Grand Designs don't suit the English. Bath Crescents and Blenheim notwithstanding, buildings in England work best when allowed to grow from below, not imported from elsewhere or imposed from above. Twisting high streets, not Haussman avenues; variegated villages, not well-planned New Towns; country houses, higgledy-piggledy and hotch-potch, not grand palaces. The buildings that sit best in the landscape are those that make best use of local materials: Devon cob, Suffolk thatch, Norfolk pantile, Cotswold stone … These are things that take centuries to develop; they can't be faked or plonked down overnight. (Sorry, Poundbury.) They are buildings that make a statement: we'll do it our way. Don't go telling us what kind of home to live in. Or, put more simply: stuff planners, sod thy neighbour.

MUSIC

As many a gap-year traveller has found to his/her cost, come party turns on that final evening, music is something that generally has the English staring at the floor in awkward embarrassment. While other nations pour forth grand choruses and soulful arias, the hapless English are left with reedy piping of the Ten Green Bottles/One Man Went to Mow/Ging-gang

Gooly Gooly/Wheels on the Bus/Hokey-Cokey variety that is, once embarked on, instantly regretted. Not having bagpipes or alpenhorn, castanets or gamelan, English music is a bit short on distinctive identity. The nearest thing to traditional folk instrument is one sheet of Izal Medicated on a scratchy comb. Hard with that to replicate the definitive sound of English Music: the wistful note of summers past, so sweetly conjured by the likes of Delius, Vaughan Williams and Elgar. People do sing in England, but they do it in the safety of the football terrace, bath or way home from the pub. The karaoke machine has much to answer for.

Elgar

POETRY

Gray's Allergy
In A Country Churchyard

Chaucer, Shakespeare, Milton, Keats, Wordsworth, Tennyson, Eliot … England has many fine poets, most of whom wrote stuff for exam boards. Generations of scholars have pored over their verse, none too sure what any of it was on about.

England's most popular poet, after Pam Ayres, was John Betjeman. From both has come poetry that is witty, sad, memorable and possible to understand. And it rhymes.

SCHOOL CONCERT, ITEM ONE:
LONDON'S BURNING

STAGE AND SCREEN

Amateur dramatics are much favoured in England. Role play, rehearsals and the final-night cast party all give cover for forms of activity not normally permitted in the suburbs. The panto season at Christmas is an added bonus, bringing tights, cross-dressing, bad jokes and thigh-slapping into the mix. Theatricals go back a long way here. When, in Elizabethan times, the Stratford Players found themselves short of men for their coming production of Ye Mousetrap, they put up a notice to advertise the part of second spear-carrier in Scenes II and IV. This caught the eye of a local youth, who dropped in a card to offer his services. 'Will shake spear,' it read on one side. The rest is mystery. Most agree that Shakespeare existed; whether or not he wrote the plays and verse that are the foundation of Eng Lit remains the subject of great debate. One school of thought has it that no non-aristocrat could have had such learning and no provincial have been so intelligent.

Hollywood Blockbusters
re-titled for English audiences:

Mission Really Not Possible If You Ask Me
Journey to the Centre of Town
Where Seagulls Dare
Meet Me In St Leonards
Apocalypse Some Time This Week-ish

SHAKESPEARE'S BIRTHPLACE

Great Weepies of Stage & Screen

America has *Gone With Wind*, of epic proportions, set amid the swirling events of the Civil War. Love, death, slavery, scandal, sherry stains, fog – they're all in there somewhere.

Europe has *La Boheme* (Mimi coughs her way round the garrets of Paris. Pavarotti sings Your Tiny Hand Is Frozen. The Christmas pressie of a muff is not enough. Mimi dies of consumption. The whole opera house reaches for its tissues).

England has *Brief Encounter*. On a railway platform, She gets a bit of coal smut in her eye. He, the doctor, steps forward. Their eyes meet across a dabbing handkerchief. Nothing further happens. Nobody runs off with anyone else. Nothing is done but the done thing. All terribly terribly. All very English.

7. Terribly Well Spoken

The English steer clear of extremism. In the land of fog and rain, it goes with the weather that things are seen not in black and white but infinite shades of grey. 'The English never draw a line without blurring it.' (Winston Churchill, 1948).

The answer is not yes or no but yes and no or possibly maybe – and then they go back on their word. Perfidious Albion. The English are happiest wobbling around the middle of the road, one wheel either side of the line.

Hyperbole is avoided; understatement is all. Well, most of it anyway. A not inconsiderable amount. 'Not bad, eh?' means 'bloody fantastic'. 'Not really my cup of tea' means 'I'd rather spend 12 days standing naked in a vat of horseshit than have to sit through that kind of thing ever again'. Politeness ordains that things aren't ever spelt out clearly but are communicated by subtle inflections, twitches of eyebrow and pile-ups of negatives. Well, hardly ever. This is where the famous stiff upper lip comes into play. Or rather, declines to play.

The English don't say what they mean or mean what they say. This can be tricky for those who do not have English as their first language. Here are some common phrases that can cause difficulty, with actual meanings alongside:

I don't mind	I do mind
I don't mind if I do	Gimme that
How are you?	Please don't reel off all your ailments
Do drop in	Next time ring, will you, so we can make our excuses and run
You're looking great	God, you've put on even more weight
Hmm, interesting . . .	You outta your mind, you crazy son of a bitch?
Just a dash	Up to the brim
Lovely to see you	Aarrgh, not again!
I'm sure you're right	I'm sure you're wrong
Bit close, eh?	You trying to kill us all by driving like that, you maniac?
I won't keep you a minute	I will keep you several minutes
A quick Jimmy Riddle	Two hours while the world falls out of my bottom
Mustn't grumble	And here's another thing that's pissing me off
With respect . . .	Pillock

USEFUL EXPRESSIONS

Well, there you go then
That's as may be
Nar-mean
And so on and so forth
Where was I?
Wossname
Thingy
Wurl
Don' ask me
Whatever
Innit
Chis-may
(cheers,
mate)

Forget regional dialect, spoken English these days falls into three categories: Youfspeak, Business-speak and Posh (employing elongated bowel sounds). Each of these is understood only by those who speak it and frequently not by them either.

Youfspeak
like cool like I waslike ohmigod whatever like

Business-speak
Dave, baby, we need to heads-up windows for blue-sky face time re orderly roll-out of interface in gap analysis noprobs . . .

Posh
git orff my land

Keep up with contemporary communication
fyi – foul up your inbox
btw – bugger, that's wrong
LOL – like ohmigod like

DOLLY PENTREATH OF MOUSEHOLE (1777)
SAID TO HAVE BEEN THE LAST NATIVE SPEAKER OF CORNISH
* Trans: 'Can you speak Cornish?'

Television has killed off regional dialect, replacing it with Australian upspeak? The faster that quaint old words fall into disuse, the more they are collected up in local books and webpages, like pinned butterflies in dusty glass cases. Go to any such list and the first thing you'll find is a local name for woodlouse, along with dialect words for hang-nail, splinter and exhaustion. Conversation in the long evenings before television revolved around fingernails, tiredness and the progress of passing woodlice. Enter Victor Meldrew.

COUNTRY WISDOM

- *You can't teach an old dog to have kittens*
- *A bird in the hand is that Marlene who serves down The Bush*
- *Don't count all your chickens in one basket without breaking eggs*
- *Good things come to those who snatch*
- *A chair unsound soon finds the ground*
- *Cast ne'er a clout till lights be out*
- *(Never remove your trousers except in the dark)*

Still fuzzy. Try going a bit to the right –

NICKNAMES

One of the penalties of being born male and English is that you may have to answer, with good grace, to a nickname not of your choosing for the rest of your days. If you happen to be tall, you will be known as Shorty, Tiny, Mini or Midge; if small, then Lofty. It's part of the English sense of humour. Those whose families may once have hailed from Ireland, Scotland or Wales can expect to be called Taffy, Jock, Paddy or Mick, in no particular order. Those with the following surnames will be saddled for life with the accompanying monicker or nickname:

Adams	Fanny	Hubbard	Mother
Bacon	Streaky	Kelly	Mother or Ned
Barker	Ronnie	Lamb	Larry
Bell	Dinger	Miller	Dusty or Windy
Bennett	Gordon	Murray	Ruby
Bird	Dicky	Murphy	Spud
Bower	Birdy	Parker	Nosey
Browning	Gravy	Riddle	Jimmy
Carpenter	Chips or Arry	Rogers	Ginger
Castle	Bouncy	Smith	Smudge
Clark	Nobby	Taylor	Tinker
Dean	Dixie	Tickell	Tess
Duckworth	Vera	Warren	Bunny
Fields	Gracie	Webb	Spider
Gordon	Flash	Wellington	Boots
Gray	Dolly	White	Chalky

Most of these lay claim to naval origin. There may not always be much to do on long trips at sea.

8. Terribly Organised

THE CHURCH OF ENGLAND

Worshippers of England have the Church of England, whose Head is the Queen. (Islanders on Tanna in the South Pacific worship the Duke of Edinburgh, though maybe less so since he started wearing that mac.) Church attendance was badly hit in the 60s, when the Forsyte Saga started appearing on Sunday evenings, and the Antiques Roadshow has not helped. Video recorders failed to halt the decline, leaving large parishes to pray for the arrival on their patch of Songs of Praise. In Victorian times churchgoers prayed for all foreigners. These days foreigners pray for the Church of England.

It is an unusual introit but they are desperate to boost attendance –

EDUCATION

Not everyone goes to Eton, of course. There's Harrow and Rugby, Radley and Roedean, Dotheboys, Winchester, Strangeways, Cheltenham Ladies' College and always St Custard's. Boarding school builds character. It stiffens the lip, thickens the hide, puts spine in the flab. For a hundred thousand pounds, spread over 4-5 years, anyone with the right background can acquire the qualities that once ran an empire: effortless superiority and a stomach able to down anything in custard or gravy. Private education (or public school, as it's called in England) does not come cheaply – similar to the costs of prison or care home – but, like these, it is a whole-life solution. Once in the system, few ever escape it.

Public schools equip their pupils with all that's needed in the world outside, giving them the skills to take charge, issue orders and be house prefect. Pupils also gain rounded vowels and a faint grasp of the Ablative Absolute. Most leavers go on to university, at Oxford, Cambridge, Bristol or Durham. (The less academic stay on at the schools that nurtured them and teach.) All then go on to interesting jobs in banking.

Networking with former members of their old school, public school products find Something in the City a necessary move in order to fund the next generation of Pidlington-Smythes entered at birth for the alma mater. However, ten years of harvesting hedge-funds and managing derivatives soon take their toll. In their 30s the bright young things of financial management are burnt out and ready to retire to the country to acquire spouse, family and 4x4, all smelling of dog.

Public school can be tough. To prepare for it, pupils spend four years away from home at preparatory school. Those needing more time to prepare can attend preparatory units from the age of three and pre-preparatory from early foetus stage.

Some people find private education just too expensive. State schools are free, but they can be noisy. Pupils in comprehensives are taught in large classes of several thousand, where they spend a number of years colouring in and doing traffic surveys, before moving on to more advanced studies in Leisure and Nailcare.

CLASS

Class in England went out of the window in the Sixties, along with bowler hats, collar studs and the Coming Out Ball. Only it didn't quite. Class lives on. It takes three people in England to change a light-bulb. One to give the order, one to do the work and one to make the tea and sweep up after. The pattern is repeated in every workplace or was till recently. These days you'd need at least another three to get the job done properly: one to do the risk assessment, one to audit the assessment and one to carry out the customer satisfaction survey. Mining, shipbuilding, farming, manufacture – all the old industries have gone, leaving most people to find work as consultants and advisors, outreach workers and facilitators, systems analysts and animators, all there to push water downhill and assist the flow of progress.

Class clings, like dogshit on a trainer. There are nooks and crannies in English life where old ways stick and can be sniffed out a mile off. And there are indicators – accents, clothing, newspapers, cars – borne by some as badges of pride and by others as burdens of birth. If these don't work, then traps and tripwires are laid across your path to check your social background. Do you say lavatory, loo or toilet? Do you have pudding or afters, dessert or sweet? Dinner or lunch, supper or tea? Lounge or living-room? Scons or scones? Do you say Cuvventry, Coventry or Coventroy? Shroesbury or Shroosbury? Is it Corrie you watch, the Archers you listen to or do you have time only for the Footsie index and racing at Ascot?

Do you say 'scones' like 'swans' or 'scones' like 'stones'?

Now test yourself. See if you can decide which class is described in each of the following:

a) Sunday afternoon at home –

Tazza and Snodge are extended on the sofa, enjoying the football over several cans of lager.

S: *Oi – hink!*
T: *Wodjamean hink?*
S: *Youblindorsomefink? Loo – hink!*
T: *Miles off.*
S: *Narnabrain.*
T: *Goal!!*
S: *Bugger, I missed it.*

b) Sunday afternoon on the family estate –

Armed with high-velocity howitzers, Roly and Staggers have taken a mixed bag of pigeon, widgeon, hedge-sparrow, gundog and peasant.

R: *One more round, then I'm orf in for sinkers and tea.*
S: *Say, bro –*
R: *Yo –*
S: *You've seen what that slimy little tick, Snibbett Minor, has gorn and done – bought out all pater's holdings in the City?*
R: *No! BANG!*
S: *Yo! BANG!*
R: *So, what do we do next?*
S: *Only one thing for it. Get Sis to marry Snibbett. BANG! BANG!*

c) Sunday afternoon in North Oxford –

'Shush,' says Mother, 'it's nearly time for me to turn on the wireless.'

With mounting excitement, Toby and Jessica stow away their trumpet and violin and skip across to the tea-table. A low buzz comes from the radiogram. It's Purtry Please, their favourite programme.

'Gumdrops,' says Toby, between mouthfuls of buttered scone,' they're doing Winthrop Mackworth Praed, my all-time fave. Would you like a hobnob, Jessica, or can I tempt you to some battenberg?'

OXFORD TRADITIONS: STUDENTS IN COLLEGE ARE LOOKED AFTER BY SCOUTS

'Walk out of a Friendly if you must, Sir Francis, but not when we're 3-1 down in a League game with Barnstaple -'

Early Times

In the beginning was lots of geology, including dinosaurs, followed eventually by the Stone Age, Stonehenge, Alfred, cakes and Ethelred the Unready. The first known inhabitants of England were cave dwellers, about whom little is known. Caves are few and far between in England, as were their early residents. These were probably people who had come into the area before the Channel was formed, moving up from an area overpopulated with cave-dwellers eg the Dordogne. They came in search of tranquillity and second homes, but found the weather wet, the neighbours surly and plumbing atrocious.

Centuries passed. Bronze and Iron Ages came and went. Romans landed, conquered and celebrated their victory as only Romans know how.

I came. I saw. I congad

King Alfred, Father of English Cookery, should not be confused with King Arthur, who may not have existed, but who died at Camlann and is buried at Glastonbury, Caerleon, Richmond, Wells, Atherstone, Alderley Edge, Anglesey, Brittany and Edinburgh. Arthur was Welsh/Scottish/Cornish/Breton (delete as applicable) but not English.

ETHELRED THE READY

Modern Times

English History gets going in 1066, when the French took over the country. Being a good loser is something much admired in England and Harold, who came second at Hastings, was no exception.

Duke William, the Bastard, went on to become, if not a great king, at least a very busy one. He built castles, dug mottes, invented round archways and conquered the land. Each evening he went round knocking on doors to find out what he had conquered and adding fresh conquests along the way. While he was inside, checking on virgates, Queen Matilda sat out in the cart, stitching on bits of Bayeux Tapestry.

All the above made William an admirable leader, but he was French. This gave rise to discontent and feuding among the barons (the Feudal System), leading on to hundreds of years of war, up to and including the Wars of the Roses. Important victories at Barnet and Tewkesbury should have enabled Yorkshire to claim the series. Instead there followed the Princes in the Tower. This dark chapter in English History came to a welcome close in 1485 with the arrival of Tudor England and Modern Times.

LESSER KNOWN FIGURES IN HISTORY:
DEREK THE CONQUEROR

Landing in Milford Haven with 1800 French troops, Henry 'Boyo' Tudor established a shiny new dynasty of major monarchs. Arguably the greatest of these was Henry VIII. Henry had six wives who rhymed; he wrote Greensleeves and threw chicken legs over his shoulder. He was succeeded by several brief but tragic reigns, including that of Nine Day Queen Lady Jane Grey, remembered only for her tea.

And this is us with that couple I told you about that we met on the boat coming into Hastings -

Then came the glorious accession of Elizabeth I, star of films and the embodiment of all that the English aspire to. She was witty, courageous, indecisive, disliked foreigners and had bad teeth. Iffy in matters of sex and religion, Elizabeth nevertheless brought a welcome sparkle to every

I know I have the body of a weak and feeble woman -

department (bar dental). Her rapier wit and over the top costumes lifted spirits sunk in gloom since the Dark Ages. One butt of her humour was Edward de Vere, Earl of Oxford, who was unfortunate enough to break wind while making a low bow to the Queen. Mortified, he fled the court and went into voluntary exile. On his return years later, according to John Aubrey, the Queen's first words to him were, 'My Lord, I had forgotten the fart.'

King Charles II, inventor of the spaniel of that name, was so taken by his canine creation that he had his hairdresser recreate the look with a full-bottomed wig that was soon all the rage. The fashion lasted long beyond the king, but these days is kept going only by High Court judges, House of Commons officials and members of the Dougal wing of the Magic Roundabout Fan Club.

' Puddles, Walter, not Poodles ! '

Once Good King Charles's golden days had come to an end, history rather lost its glamour. In came the Industrial Revolution, trailing clouds of smoke and steam. Within just a few generations the population went from rural to urban, from manual labour to clickers of mouse. History ended; in came the future.

ENGLAND EXPECTS

ENGLISH INVENTORS

England takes pride in its inventors and their contributions to civilisation, from Stephen Perry (rubber band, 1845) to Sir Clive Sinclair (the legendary C5). Rubber bands have been a lasting boon to children wishing to ping things in maths lessons; they also provide work for Royal Mail personnel, employed to scatter these on pavements in residential areas. Ahead of Perry was Thomas Hancock, who patented elastic fastening for suspenders in 1820. While his younger brother Walter was out building steam buses, Thomas Hancock, inventor of the masticator, put all his efforts into rubber. In the end he teamed up with Charles Macintosh to develop waterproof raincoats that might so easily have been called Hancocks instead (and cinemas filled with Dirty Hancocks).

William Addis, in prison at the time, lays claim to the first mass-produced toothbrush (1780). Made of cowhair and bone, it may have been a bit on the big side (the Addis Company went on to find many other uses for their brushes), but it was an improvement on what went before. That was mopping teeth with a rag dipped in salt and soot (for whitening).

Another techno wizard was Edwin Beard Budding of Stroud, inventor of both the lawnmower and the adjustable spanner. The one gave rise to the other. For more on lawnmowers, visit the National Lawnmower Museum in Shakespeare St, Southport, Lancs, which houses a fine display of mower manuals along with clipping machines of the rich and famous (Hilda Ogden, Vanessa Feltz and Diana, Princess of Wales). It also has the largest toy lawnmower collection in the world.

No account of inventors would be complete without mention of Frank Hornby (Meccano, 1901). When the Dambuster raids took place over Germany in 1943, their bombing runs were worked out on an analogue computer (Differential Analyser No 2) built mainly of Meccano. Shades of England's all-time greatest inventor, William Heath Robinson.

THINGS CAN ONLY GET BETTER

Things that aren't as good as they used to be –

> Royal Mail/postal system
> Post Offices
> hedgerows
> servants

Inventor Arnold Pimbley demonstrates his early Prototype TV Remote Control

Things that have got better –

stamps that don't need licking (but not so good if you're a collector)

10. Terribly Down To Earth

England is part of Europe only in the sense that it's not part of Africa, Asia or Antarctica. Europe to the English is over there and across the water. It's somewhere to travel to on holiday. It's foreign, with people and food to be regarded with equal suspicion. Europe is everything England is not: stylish, sophisticated and good at football. Occasionally England chooses to stand shoulder to shoulder with partners in Europe, Harris Tweed brushing awkwardly against smooth Armani. But for the most part England stands aloof, proud of its position midway between Europe and America, and roughly in line with Iceland, the Azores and Tristan da Cunha.

The UK has much the same sized population as France but in less than half the space. That's why you're twice as likely to bump into someone this side of the Channel. At 1,010 per sq mile (or 395 per sq km) England has pretty much the densest population in Europe (due to overtake the Netherlands in two years and then be second only to Malta).

Down the centre of the country runs England's backbone, the Pennine Chain. Like the Jacobite Rebellion of 1745, this peters out round Derby, leaving the south of England soft and spineless. The North was settled by Angles, the South by Saxons. The main difference between them was (and is) in their vowels. The Angles would run a bath (bath like 'Kath' and run like 'full') and cut the grass (like 'foot' and 'lass'). Saxons would runn a barth and cutt the grarss. Or get a little man down the road to do it for them.

since Nelson fell at Trafalgar. Osborne House, Queen Victoria's home on the Isle of Wight, has a large fresco recording this fact. Painted by Dyce in 1847, it is titled 'Neptune Resigning to Britannia the Empire of the Sea'.

People in England make regular trips to the seaside to keep an eye on the waters they own and check it's all there. Armed with Sunday papers and thermos, they are to be found staring out of parked cars all round the coastline, watching and waiting for something to happen. Then there are the activists who unfold and inflate whole homes and gardens of flapping plastic and swishing terylene, complete with fences and flags to proclaim their rights of possession.

Strict rules of protocol govern the take-up of positions on any beach. In claiming a spot to call your own, you must be exactly midway between encampments on either side and out of earshot. If this is not possible, you must trudge on with your possessions beyond the furthest settlement until such a place is found. There are families that set off round the coastline never to be seen again.

There are two types of beachgoer. Type A, bearing a minimum of possessions in one small envelope, settles on the sand to switch off from the world and turn gently brown, while tides and empires rise and fall. Type B, bored and irritable after 3.9 seconds of sandcastle-building, cricket, French cricket, boules, sandcastle-bombing and tea, somehow manages also to be bitten by insects, savaged by seaweed, lacerated by molluscs, widdled on by dogs, burnt by the sun, hit in the face by a cricket ball and garotted by next-door's kite. There is usually one of each type in each family.

Seaside resorts also fall into two categories: genteel and vulgar. Brighton & Hove, Clacton & Frinton, Southend & Leigh, Margate and Westgate, Sandown & Shanklin ... If in doubt, a quick call to the local Tourist Board will enable you to find the correct place for someone of your background and social standing.

THE WEATHER

The most important thing in England – more so even than money, sex, health or football – is the weather. The English have 72 different words for rain. Weather varies. It varies from hour to hour, season to season, place to place. This fundamental truth never ceases to amaze the English. 'Not like it was this morning,' they'll say, with genuine surprise. 'Bit of a change from yesterday.' 'Glad we're not up in Scotland!'

The English tend not to converse, not in the south of England anyway and not if they're strangers. The weather is the one ground on which this rule may be broken. It is the opening move to all forms of communication and intercourse. Foreigners kiss, dogs sniff bums, English people exchange observations on the weather. Usually these are statements of the bleeding obvious. If the clouds pass and sun comes out, they will point this out to complete strangers in the street, adding by way of explanation,

'Look, sun!' And if it's raining or hot or cold or mild or foggy or grey, they'll turn to each other and say, 'Ugh, raining!', 'Phew, hot!', 'Brrr, cold!', 'Hmm, mild!' Kerrumphblahdunglecrump. 'Gosh, thunder!'. In every case, the correct response is one of confirmation and agreement; this leaves the door swinging open to further discussion and analysis, depending on the tone of voice in which the rejoinder is delivered. Usually a brief exchange suffices. Feelers have been put out, an alliance established and the railway journey or wait at the bus-stop can continue another five hours in comfortable silence. The wrong form of reply is to contradict and deny.

HOW SOUTHERNERS TEND TO THINK OF THE NORTH

In fact most people in England don't care a toss about the weather; they've got used to it. Weather conversations are just part of the vetting procedure. Meet in the street, be trapped in a lift, share the same nuclear bunker – first act must be to pass comment on the state of weather for the time of year. Obtain agreement and all parties can immediately see they are on the same wavelength and safe to proceed with. Further agree that the forecast was wrong and bonding is complete. Fail to pick up the signals or return the right password and the relationship breaks down.

Conversation about the weather is safe ground for all but foreigners who do not know the rules of the game. 'Cold, eh?' comes the cheery opening gambit. 'No,' replies the foreigner, with fatal honesty. (Correct response: blooming freezing). Try again. 'Look, it's raining.' Incorrect answer: 'Yes, I can see that.' (Correct response: not what they forecast, is it?)

The English are happy discussing the weather. It's not like philosophy, which baffles them, or fashion (ditto). It is safe ground, on which agreement can easily be reached.

11. Gazetteer

North West	– Cumbria, Lancashire, Cheshire
North East	– Northumberland, Durham, Yorkshire
W Midlands	– Shropshire, Staffordshire, Warwickshire
E Midlands	– Derbyshire, Nottinghamshire, Leicestershire, Lincolnshire, Rutland, Northamptonshire
E Anglia	– Norfolk, Suffolk, Essex, Cambridgeshire, Huntingdonshire, Bedfordshire
West	– Hereford/Worcestershire, Gloucestershire, Oxfordshire, Wiltshire
Home Counties	– Berkshire, Buckinghamshire, Hertfordshire, Middlesex
South East	– London, Kent, Surrey, Sussex
South West	– Hampshire, Dorset, Somerset, Devon, Cornwall

NORTH WEST – CUMBRIA, LANCASHIRE, CHESHIRE

Cumbria

Home to: Ackenthwaite, Crackenthorpe, Gubbergill, Pica, Corkickle, Warblebank, Blawith and Subberthwaite, Durdar, Dubbs, Bog, Stank, Oughterby, Outcast, Whamtown, Thiefside, Quality Corner, Meathop and Ulpha, Bewaldeth & Snittlegarth, Bothel & Thrupland, Birker with Austhwaite, Rottington, Trough, Cumrew Outside & Inside, Blencogo, Barfs

noted for: pencils, mint cake, writers, fells, wrestling, daffodils

Chiefly known these days as an over-eager breed of sausage, Cumberland used to be a county in its own right, along with Westmorland. Then came boundary changes in 1974 and the two got lumped together, with bits of Lancashire, to form Cumbria. Or not – if you are the sort that likes to stick with the name of the county you were born into.

Cumbria has England's highest peak (Scafell Pike). It also has its largest lake (Windermere), its deepest lake (Wastwater), its straightest lake (Coniston), its most beautiful lake (Ullswater), its most remote lake (Ennerdale Water), alternatively its most beautiful lake (Derwent Water), its steepest road (Wrynose – Hard Knott Pass), its finest traffic jams (Windermere), its largest pencil (Keswick), its best views (Helvellyn), its oldest rounders field (Castlerigg), its best laxative (standing beneath the Bowder Stone), its most popular climb (Skiddaw) and its best selection of jigsaws (Grasmere). And it has the biggest liars (annual competition at Wasdale).

local lingo: Cumbrian Chat (also the name of an online dating agency)
as in: Owz it gan? Ahreet.

Lancashire

home to: Bickerstaffe, Back o' Bowley, Burrow-with-Burrow, Brunshaw Bottom, Barnacre with Bonds, Dawber Delf, Deeply Vale, Great Crimbles, Fiddlers Ferry, Huttock End, Tootle Height, Town Bent, Weston with Preese, Scronkey, Snodworth, Ribby with Wrea, Nether Burrow, Slyne with Hest, Midge Hall, Little Eccleston with Larbreck, Huntroyde Demesne, York, Knott End on Sea

noted for: cotton, lasses, hotpot, eccles cakes, lobby, Willy Eckerslike, Fisherman's Friends, Victory Vs, Chorley cakes, throdkins

Gone are the clogs and shawls, gone the cobbles and mills and gone is Ena Sharples. Gone, too, are Liverpool and Manchester, now independent unitary authorities, grown up and flown the nest. Lancashire isn't quite the same as when Lowry was painting little figures, our Gracie was singing down the alley and George Formby out leaning on lamp-posts. Not everything has gone from the Good Old Days; they still have Blackpool, they still have the Pleasure Beach and they still have good old sewage in the sea. Aka Mersey goldfish.

They like their nibbles in Lancashire. Blackpool Rock (thicker and redder than that of its rivals) is said to owe its development to Dynamite Dick of Morecambe. Eccles Cakes and Chorley Cakes are closely related, similar but different; a close cousin, down on its luck, is the Sad Cake, also known as Desolate Cake (or Tragic, if no sign of currant). The county's signature dish is Lancashire Hot Pot, which, according to the county's official website for tourism, is a simple peasant dish. Take one simple peasant; add potato and onion.

local lingo: Lanky / Lankie Twang
as in: as in: owdo, appen, al'reet, gradely, wossup-withi, sawreetferthee, champion, na then, theer, cratchy, nobbut, tha'sen, mi'sen, flunter, ottymotty

Liverpool

There is much debate about the origin of the name Liverpool, variously ascribed. The ending '-pool' may come from the Welsh 'pwll', meaning 'pool'. Once known as the 'Second City of the Empire', Liverpool remains famous for Beatles, poets, football and ferries across the Mersey.

local lingo: Scouse
      as in: Lens a fiver, Yew up fer wann?

Manchester

Manchester, like Liverpool, is famous for popstars and football and, like Birmingham, it is the UK's Second City (tell that to Cardiff, Edinburgh or Belfast). Once Cotton was King; now it's Corrie and Culture. Annual rainfall in Manchester is below the national average – official.

local lingo: Manc
      as in: youse, madferit, our kid, buzzin, down our end

Cheshire

home to: Cuckoos Nest, Antrobus, Checkley cum Wrinehill, Dodcott cum Wilkesley, Benty Heys, Bratts Bank, Husseys Nook, Tottys Hill, Vicars Cross, Marlston cum Lache, Mossley Moss, Soss Moss, Shavington cum Gresty, Pott Shrigley, Peover Inferior, Shocklach Oviatt, Ankers Knowl, The Bongs, Aston juxta Mondrum

noted for: cheese, salt, footballers' wives, black-and-white buildings

Alderley Edge, Tarporley, Prestbury, Altrincham ... Cheshire (anagram: riches, eh) these days has its Golden Triangle and connotations with affluence. But not all in the county is nouveau or riche. The county name comes from historic, walled Chester, itself named after a Roman stronghold and scattered still with fine remains, from huge amphitheatre to the hypocaust system that lurks in the basement of Spudulike on Bridge St. Unique to Chester are the ancient Rows, with probably the oldest shop-front in England (claim disputed by an early 12th cent Allied Carpets sale front in Luton). By ancient law Welshmen are prohibited from entering Chester after dark.

Cheshire has the only working salt mine in England; down it are sent to work those who contravene the fashion codes of Knutsford and Wilmslow.

local lingo: Cheshire

as in: twarly, tossicated, frabbly, trollock, yawky, whabble, whabbock, thruggil, thrummel, spadger, spectables, sniddlebog, nuddle off, mulligrubs, feyther

NORTH EAST – NORTHUMBERLAND, DURHAM, YORKSHIRE

Northumberland

home to: Harbottle, Larbottle, Oh Me Edge, Wae's Me, Mohope Moor, Dirt Pot, Slaggyford, Humshaugh, Ogle, Kitty Brewster, Isabella Pit, Wide Open, Kirkwhelpington, Knogley, Snitter, Snod's Edge, New York, Once Brewed, Twice Brewed, Adderstone with Lucker, Amble by the Sea

noted for: coast and moor, pipes, brass bands, castles, Farnes, Charltons, Grace Darling, Pete Doherty

At the northernmost point of Northumberland is Berwick on Tweed, which has changed hands between England and Scotland more times than most people can remember (14 at the last count). When the Crimean War broke out, the declaration was made in this country on behalf of Britain, Ireland, British Dominions and Berwick upon Tweed. When peace was made, two years on, they forgot the last bit and Berwick continued a lonely war with Russia for 110 years. This ended in 1966 with a small ceremony attended by a Soviet official to the relief of all.

Northumberland used to have Newcastle upon Tyne as its county town, but that got snaffled in 1974, along with Gateshead and Sunderland from County Durham, to make up Tyne & Wear. That leaves the title of county town as cause of argument between Morpeth and Alnwick.

local lingo: Northumbrian

Tyne & Wear

Geordie is the term loosely used for anyone from the North East and/or the language they speak (aa's gannin doon toon). But, for purists, a Geordie has to have been born within spitting distance of the Tyne, while proper Geordie talk is totally different from that of their neighbours – Mackems of Sunderland, Smoggies of Teesside, Monkey Hangers of Hartlepool. In Newcastle they say Haway; on Wearside it's Howay. In Geordie, 'we' becomes 'wi'; in Mackem it's 'wuh' – and 'who' becomes 'wee'. However, differences are less marked these days, thanks to the influence of television and fillum.

Durham

home to: Pity Me, Wham, Lynesack and Softley, Fondly Set, Wackerfield, Ruffside, Lumley Thicks, Quaking Houses, Cassop cum Quarrington, Toronto, Quebec, Canada, Philadelphia, Dabble Duck, Foggy Furze, No Place, Croxdale and Hett, Binchester Blocks, Branden and Byshottles, Whitworth Without

noted for: railways, galas, Singin' Hinnies,

County Durham is nicely set out. It's the way you would do it yourself, if starting off with a clean sheet of paper and pocket set of geographical features. You'd begin with a good run of coastline, marked off between two big rivers to act as county boundaries; the fourth side you'd close off with a line of hills, from which the rivers flow. Across the middle of the county you would run a third, more interesting river, meandering with kinks. Roughly midway along you'd put the county town, centring it on one such kink, where the river winds round a rocky height. (The city's founders in AD 995 came to the same conclusion, with the help of divine intervention; they were carrying the coffin of St Cuthbert at the time and following the directions of a milkmaid in search of her missing dun cow.) On top of this you would put your cathedral, along with a castle, why not. Being of sound northern temperament, you would site the whole lot about as far from London as can be. That's Durham. All right, pretty much the same could be said for each and every one of England's eastern counties. It's a system that works and Durham does it best of all.

local lingo: Pitmatic / Pitmatical (dialect used by Durham miners – extensive vocabulary, if somewhat coal-related.)

chinglees

[marble-sized coal]

brat

[inferior coal]

Yorkshire

home to: Agglesthorpe, Wigglesworth, Wetwang, Lumbutts, Fangfoss, Thwing, Whaw, Crackpot, Damems, Swine, Gribthorpe, Grimethorpe, Flush Dyke, Idle, Eight and Forty, Land of Nod, Ainderby Quernhow, Thornton le Beans, Newby Wiske, Danby Wiske, Great Heck, Blubberhouses, Totties, Thick Hollins, Merrybent, Sexhow, Booze, Landmoth cum Catto, Corker Bottoms, Kirkby Overthrow, Noon Nick, Upperthong, Netherthong, Dalby cum Skewsby, Cridling Stubbs, Meanly, Potto, Jump, Booze, Grewelthorpe, Little Fryup, Wombleton, Sprotbrough and Cusworth, Allerton Mauleverer with Hoppe, Bilsdale Midcable, Nova Scotia, Thorngumbald, Buttercrambe with Bossall, Illton cum Pott, Acaster Malbis, Throstle Bower, Squirrel Ditch, Thirkleby, Little Thirkleby, Robin Hood, Bilton in Ainsty with Bikerton, Eskdaleside cum Ugglebarnby, Kettlesing Bottom

noted for: Brontes, dales, terriers, the Leeds/Bradford writer/artist David Alan Hockney Bennett, parkin, pikelets, pudding, gumption, the smell in the Jorvik Centre

also noted for home-grown products, including Yorkshire tea (grown on south facing slopes of high moorland), rhubarb, licorice & chocolate oranges. Equally notable, the Denby Dale Pie, baked in the S Yorkshire village on special occasions (nine in all) since the first, served up in 1788 to celebrate George III's return from madness. That of 1846 (marking the Repeal of the Corn Laws), was 8 ft across and contained 100 lbs of beef, 1 calf, 5 sheep, 21 rabbits/hares and 89 game-birds/poultry. Sadly, all this got trampled underfoot as the crowd of 15,000 surged forward to get a piece and the stage collapsed beneath them. Its successor of 1887 (Victoria's Golden Jubilee) fared no better; bigger and better than all before, this one's contents went off most foully, releasing noxious fumes on cooking, and the whole thing was buried, with funeral rites, in a massive lime-pit.

Yorkshire is Yorkshire, God's Own County and all that. Stretching from Whernside (736 m) to Hull (highest point 11 m above sea level), Yorkshire remains England's largest historic county and a law unto itself. It has resisted all attempts to dismantle and divide into ridings or regions. All that ever mattered to a Yorkshireman in the past (before the modification of the birth qualification rule in 1992) was to have been born within the bounds of the county and so be eligible, when the call came, to don cricket-pads for Yorkshire. Yorkshire folk are 'tykes' and proud of it; you can tell a Yorkshireman, but you can't tell him anything.

Back in Roman times, Eboracum (or, in Yorkshire, Ee Boracum) was joint capital of Britain and in the time of Emperor Septimus Severus the whole Roman Empire was run by him from there. And, in the eyes of the locals, that's how things have stayed.

Yorkshire motto (unofficial): If tha does owt for nowt, do it for thysen.
Yorkshire motto (official): Nay lad, tha's doing that all wrong.

local lingo: Tyke (which differs in every town in Yorkshire), Yammer
as in: Eyup, tha knows, a reight gooid sooart

W MIDLANDS – SHROPSHIRE, STAFFORDSHIRE, WARWICKSHIRE

Shropshire

home to: Bitterley, Booley, Bedlam, Bings, Sodylt Bank, Crudgington, Grimpo, Diddlebury, Dudddlewick, Twitchen, Tong, Quatt, Quabbs, Hopton Wafers, Wyken, Wykey, Aqueduct, Battlefield, Chemistry, Lubberland, Preston Gubbals, New Invention, Gobowen, The Werps, The Wintles, The Bog, Ruyton XI Towns, Asterley Pontesford, Worthen with Shelve

noted for: lads

Famous folk of Shropshire include Charles Darwin, Wilfrid Owen and Abraham Darby I-III. Also listed are Edric the Wild, Mad Jack Mytton (Regency rake) and Roy Wood of Wizard, who came from Wem.

Shropshire can be abbreviated to Salop, which is short for Salopesberia, if that helps. The county is rich in castles, green space and blue remembered hills: The Wrekin, The Long Mynd, Wenlock Edge ... The area around Church Stretton has been known since Victorian times as Little Switzerland. Quite little, though.

local lingo: Shrops Talk / Spake Salop
as in: Come thy ways in, tak your 'ook

TRADITIONAL GREETINGS OF SHREWSBURY

Staffordshire

home to: Acton Trussell, Baggots Bromley, Crackley, Loggerheads, Draycott in the Clay, Seedy Mill, Hints, The Wergs, Tatenhill Tixall, Tittesworth, Heath Hayes and Wimblebury, Weston under Lizard

noted for: Potteries, breweries, bull terriers, the Reliant Robin and Flash (at 1518 ft, the highest placed village in Britain)

What with the flumes and Black Hole of Stoke on Trent's Waterworld, Adrenalin Tubing at Tamworth's Snow Dome, the Apocalypse tower drop at Drayton Manor Theme Park and the 125-odd rides at Alton Towers, Staffordshire offers more ways of making you throw up than almost all other counties put together. Alton Towers was originally the home of the Earls of Shrewsbury, who had their own versions of Nemesis, Oblivion and Cloud Cuckoo Land.

In 1902 the first jar of Marmite in the world was produced in the county, at Burton upon Trent. That's the kind of snippet of information you either love or hate.

local lingo: Black Country talk (Yam Yam from 'Yow Am') in Dudley area, NW of Birmingham, towards Wolverhampton, not to be confused with Brummie (similar words, diff pron) – Ow b'ist?

as in: Owa(r)mya? Bay too bah (I'm not too bad). Yow big lommock .

Birmingham

Good old Brum, at the heart of the West Midlands, is England's second city and one-time 'workshop of the world'. Custard powder was invented here, as was the Balti curry. Birmingham has more miles of canal than Venice, but fewer cruise-ships visiting.

local lingo: Brummie

as in: Adu (How are you?) Anyroadup, flower (floor), dower (door)

Places round Birmingham
Andzwuff, Broily Eel, Cassill Brummich, Digbuff, Ockloy, Oiters Eef, Orl Groin, Yardloy, Suttin Codefoiled, Wolve-ram-tin

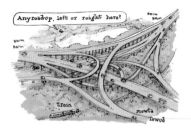

Warwickshire

home to: Haseley Knob, Foul End, Bishops Itchington, Dagtail End, Barnacle, Bermuda, Kites Hardwick, Snitterfield, Tattle Bank, Norton Curlieu, Harborough Parva, Little Britain, Radford Semele, Sutton under Brailes, Wagon Overthrow, Weston under Wetherley, Baddesley Clinton, Pillerton Priors

noted for: Shakespeare, Forest of Arden, absence of forest, doubts about Shakespeare

Henry James, in 1905, described Warwickshire as 'the core and centre of the English world; midmost England, unmitigated England.'

Warwickshire is still at the heart of England (or, at least, England and Wales), even if it is no longer the neat shape it once was. Boundary changes in 1974 took out Birmingham, Coventry and Solihull, leaving the county looking pretty hacked off on the map.

Sir Guy of Warwick was famous from the 12-13th century for fighting dragons, giants and great boar and for slaying the Dun-cow of Dunsmore. Warwick Castle holds his sword and his porridge pot; as the county's tourist board can't help commenting, the survival of these relics is miraculous, as Sir Guy himself never existed.

local lingo: Warwickshire
as in: Worro, A do

E MIDLANDS – DERBYSHIRE, LEICESTERSHIRE, NOTTINGHAMSHIRE, LINCOLNSHIRE, RUTLAND, NORTHAMPTONSHIRE

Derbyshire

home to: Ault Hucknall, Eckington, Arkwright Town, Bugsworth, Conksbury, Cackleton Green, Calling Low, Cock Alley, Denby Bottles, Dobholes, Dimple, Dinting Vale, Nether End, Hoon Hay, Oxton Rakes, Glutton Bridge, Hungry Bentley, Robin Hood, Scarthin Nick, Hartington Nether Quarter, Spout, Shottle and Postern, Tinkersick, Toadhole Furnace, Kinder Downfall, Goodwins Lumbs

noted for: Brian Clough, rams, Joan, Bakewell, tart

Derbyshire is bang in the middle of England and about as far from the sea as you get. It makes up for this by having rivers, dales and peaks that, for scenic attraction, knock spots off the likes of Eastbourne or Worthing. Such delights in the past were not always accessible to the working-classes, not unless employed as gamekeepers – not, that is, until the famous Kinder Trespass of 1932. Hundreds of militant ramblers amassed, from Manchester and around, to storm the open but not open moorland. Scuffles ensued and six walkers were nobbled by the police on their way down, ending up in prison for riotous assembly (convicted, it was said, by a jury of landowning ex-army officers). But it was a landmark event, which played a key part in the opening up of National Parks and Right to Roam. On the 70th anniversary of the event, the then Duke of Devonshire had the grace to speak out, formally apologising for the attitude of his grandfather.

Derbyshire folk are practical types, not given to mankin' abaht. Derbyshire is home to engineering.

local lingo: Derbyshire Drawl

as in: Rayt, is it woth ote? It's nowt te dow wi' mey

Peak District: Ahm pigged off. Athagonnabrewupthen?

Nottinghamshire

home to: Bunny, Bogend, Blidworth Bottoms, Cropwell Bishop, Cropwell Butler, Barnby in the Willows, Sturton le Steeple, Watnall Cantelupe, Weecar, Willoughby in the Wolds, Barton in Fabis, North Leverton with Habblesthorpe, Rhodesia, Perlethorpe cum Budby, Zouch

noted for: Sheriff of Nottingham, Sherwood Forest, cycles, chemists, Lady Chatterley's Lover

In its list of Famous Nottinghamshire People, the Information Britain website includes Dale Winton, Graham Taylor and Harold Shipman – along with Lord Byron, Jesse Boot and DH Lawrence (famous last words, 'I am getting better'). Robin Hood, the county's most famous son, may never have existed or, if he did, may well have come from Yorkshire. Try telling that to the people of Notts.

Nottingham was originally Snottingham.

local lingo: Notts
as in: Worrizzit? Gizzit ear. Gizza gozz (let's have a look).

Leicestershire

home to: Gumley, Glooston, Hugglescote, Snibston, Sheepy Magna, Frisby on the Wreake, Peatling Parva, Barton in the Beans, Newtown Unthank, Willoughby Waterleys, Long Clawson, Norton juxta Twycross, Nanpantan, Botcheston, Illston on the Hill

noted for: pies, crisps, Stilton, Red Leicester, the National Space Centre, socks

(Stilton, by law, can only be made in the counties of Leics, Derbys, Notts, though it takes its name from a place in Cambs where the cheese was never made.)

Leics CC coat of arms is supported by a black bull and a Leicestershire ram, of equal size, that you wouldn't want to meet on a dark night. Across the top runs a 'fox courant over stubble proper' – a nod in the direction of Hugo Meynell of Quorn or of Leicester City Football Club. The arms are quartered and show a five-leaved plant, a lion with two tails, a black sleeve and something that resembles a used condom. It's an ostrich feather (or emu plume, whichever it is they have in Leics). The motto is *For'ard, For'ard*.

local lingo: Leicester
     as in: croaker (doctor), chuddies (underpants, Hinglish), Ay up me duck

Lincolnshire

home to: Carlton Scroop, Cowbit, Burton Coggles, Dyke, Old Leake, New York, Friskney Eaudike, Pywipe, Wasps Nest, Ashby Puerorum, Limber Parva, Grange de Lings, Mavis Enderby, Yaddlethorpe, Sots Hole, Grimblethorpe, Stragglethorpe, Donna Nook, Toft next Newton, Newton by Toft, Aby, Orby, Irby, Atterby, Utterby, Brattleby, Belchford, Thimbleby, Dembleby, Snitterby, Strubby, Fockerby, Legsby, Spital in the Street

noted for: imps, poachers, dykes, Margaret Thatcher

Not all of Lincolnshire lies under water, or 'watter', as they say in the north of the county. Wolds Top, high in the Wolds, soars to 551 ft (168m). But, between Humber and Wash, Carrs and Fen, a good deal of Lincs is either coastline battered by sea or land reclaimed from the sea and criss-crossed by ditches and drains (dryeeaairns). 10 sq km of the county is under sea-level. Lincolnshire folk are known as Yeller Bellies and the county's most famous son (give or take Tennyson) was Isaac Newton.

local lingo: Lincolnshire
       as in: Now then (hello), daft as a boiled owl

Rutland

home to: Edith Weston, Thistleton, Stoke Dry, Thorpe by Water

noted for: horseshoes, and for being mostly under Rutland Water

Rutland lays claim to being England's smallest county, a claim hotly disputed by the Isle of Wight at high tide.

Northamptonshire

home to: Easton Maudit, Blatherwyke, Bozeat, Bengal, Nobottle, Newbottle, Hinton in the Hedges, Hanging Houghton, Yardley Gobion, Duddington with Fineshade, Forceleap, Slapton, Supton, Snorscomb, Woodford cum Membris.

noted for: shoes, spires, canals, squires and the World Conker Championships in Ashton

Included in the website listings of Famous People from Northamptonshire are Ebenezer Prout, Jim Dale, Thomas Tresham I, Thomas Tresham II, Norton Strange Townshend, two football referees and Arthur Mold, 'one of the deadliest fast bowlers of his day' (Wikipedia). But none can really match the greatness of 'peasant poet' John Clare, whose pastoral evocations of the county (all thistledown and throstles – 'the sleepy rustic sloomy goes') were penned long before Corby New Town came into being.

Northamptonshire shares a boundary with Lincolnshire just 19 metres long.

local lingo: Northamptonshire
as in: Ay yup. Yis, m'ole boodie.
Moynd yersalf .

E ANGLIA – NORFOLK, SUFFOLK, ESSEX, CAMBRIDGESHIRE, HUNTINGDONSHIRE, BEDFORDSHIRE

Norfolk

home to: Cake Street, Cats Bottom, Noddle Corner, Sloley, California, Philadelphia, Quebec, Brow of the Hill, Ivy Todd, Alby with Thwaite, Daffy Green, Little Snoring, Great Snoring, Puddledock, Piccadilly Corner, Waterloo, St Helena, Ormesby St Margaret with Scratby, Seething, Stratton Strawless, Trunch.

noted for: dumplings, Broads, broads, Broad Norfolk, Delia.
County motto: One up on Suffolk

'Very flat, Norfolk,' said Noel Coward, but then he never cycled the county. And he meant it metaphorically. Those who have not been there picture Norfolk as bog and fen; that's Lincolnshire or Cambs – only the bogs vanished centuries back, when the fens were drained, leaving rivers banked up high above the surrounding land. Small boys from Holland are flown in at times of emergency.

As its many ancient churches testify, Norfolk was once a place of fabulous wealth, nowadays confined to the Golden Triangle twixt Burnham and Holt. (Norwich has its own Golden Triangle, as do Los Angeles, India and the opium-producing areas of South-East Asia.)

Norfolk people speak in an accent impossible to replicate on television or radio, or not since the days of Boy John and the Singing Postman. Instead, actors make do with a blend of Mummerset and Borset, with flourishes of Welsh thrown in for good measure. While the Welsh are not known for their reticence, Norfolk people rarely speak and, if they do, keep utterances down to one word or two. The second one is 'off'. It's the East wind that does it.

local lingo: Broad Norfolk (not to be confused with Norfuk, the blend of English and Tahitian which is the co-official language of Norfolk Island in the South Pacific)

as in: Cor blarst me. That'll larn yer. She coont larn me nuffin.

Suffolk

home to: Charles Tye, Honey Tye, Hoo, Culpho, Dallinghoo, Nedging Tye, Rickinghall Superior, Rickinghall Inferior, Reydon Smear, Cuckolds Green, Nedging with Naughton, Thurston Planch, Onehouse, Bradfield Combust with Stannin, Great Wratting

noted for: Thomas Gainsborough, John Constable, Benjamin Britten and Dani Filth of the black metal band Cradle of Filth.

East of Ipswich in 1980 was where the famous Rendlesham Forest Incident occurred on 26 December with the landing of a UFO in woods close to two air bases in use at the time by the USAF. Or it was the beam of Orford Ness lighthouse bouncing off the clouds. Or servicemen in the area having a good Christmas.

local lingo: Suffolk

as in: valeration, pollywiggle, appletite, siggify, cotterage

WORDS CONFOOSED IN NORFOLK AND SUFFOLK

Essex

home to: Barking, Fobbing, Mucking, Buttsbury, Foulness, Duck End, Cock Clarks, Coblers Green, Ugley, Gubbions Green, Matching Tye, Pouches, Maggots End, Beaumont cum Moze, New Thundersley, Common Side, Steeple Bumpstead, Shellow Bowells, Puttock End

noted for: Lakeside Shopping Centre, Bluewater Shopping Centre

Essex is a county of contrasts. Think Essex and you might be forgiven for thinking first urban and modern: Essex girl, New Towns (Basildon, Harlow), shopping and concrete, Dagenham and Romford. But Essex also does old and green: Thaxted and Hedingham, Audley End, Coggeshall, Saffron Walden. Bradwell Chapel (ad 654) is reckoned to be the oldest church in England and Colchester the oldest town on record. Great Bentley has the largest village green in the country and Finchingfield (with its duckpond, cottages, windmill, church and footbridge over the Pant) the most photographed. Essex has too some of the wildest, least visited and muddiest coastline in England.

local lingo: Estuary
　　　as in: sumfink else, doancha, innit

TEMPUST

OWD STARMCHER

SNARTH

CLUNG

SLUDDY BUSKINS

ESSEX STILE

ESSEX, OLD ...

Innit

EFFING FOREST

... AND NEW

Cambridgeshire

home to: Westley Waterless, Six Mile Bottom, Gimbers End, Grunty Fen, Queen Adelaide, America, Prickwillow, Ramsey Forty Foot, Bassingbourn cum Kneesworth, Shingay cum Wendy

noted for: World Pea Shooting Championships (held each year at Witcham nr Ely)

Also noted for a university. Cambridge is not the country's oldest university. That honour goes to Oxford; but it was bad relations between town and gown that caused scholars in 1209 to flee Oxford for Cambridge. In Cambridge the trouble continued. Early records of the University are dotted with references to hostility and friction in that place too. You'd have thought they might have learnt something by then. The motto of the University is *Hinc lucem et pocula sacra*. This translates as 'From this place, light and sacred draughts'. Or 'Light up here and devoted drinking'.

local lingo: Fen
as in: slub (mud), retch (allotted patch for pulling carrots etc), docky (snack lunch), hunch (chunk of bread)

CAMBRIDGE ALL-STARS
WARMING UP FoR THE BIG ONE v OXFORD

Huntingdonshire

home to: Pidley, Hail Weston, Pidley Fen, Molesworth

noted for: Oliver Cromwell, John Major, being swallowed up by Cambridgeshire

Huntingdonshire was annexed by Cambridgeshire in 1974, but it was a takeover peacefully achieved, without use of tanks. St Neots was named after the diminutive saint (just 4 ft tall) who, tradition has it, was nevertheless related to Alfred the Great and who went on to become the patron saint of fish.

Huntingdonshire Day: April 25th

local lingo: Standard English – the local dialect of Hunts, together with neighbouring Beds and Northants, was the basis for one of the first forms of Standard English to emerge in the 14th century. Garn wiv yer. True.

WEEKEND TRAINING EXERCISE FOR MEMBERS OF
THE FENLAND MOUNTAIN RESCUE TEAM

Bedfordshire

home to: Milton Ernest, Souldrop, Barton in the Clay, Top End, Up End, Turvey, Ireland, Moggerhanger, Heath and Reach, Hundred of Willey, Backnoe End, Limbury cum Biscot

Poor old Bedfordshire: in the middle of everywhere, but not part of anywhere. It's not in the Midlands, it's not really East Anglia and it's certainly not Hame Carnties. Until recently there were road signs at the county boundary bearing the words,' Welcome to Bedfordshire, Central to the Oxford-Cambridge Arc'. Next door to somewhere nicer. But then a good many English people have made their homes in parts of

Bedfordshire, insofar as much of the county was scooped out in former times as clay by the London Brick Company for new houses in all parts. Stewartby was once the world's largest brickworks.

local lingo: Bedfordshire
  as in: gudgel (hole of stagnant water), soodle (saunter), mulluk (litter)

goolabee   soodle
mulluk
gudgel

WEST – HEREFORDSHIRE, WORCESTERSHIRE, GLOUCESTERSHIRE, OXFORDSHIRE, WILTSHIRE

Herefordshire

home to: Ocle Pychard, Moreton on Lugg, Ashford Bowdler, Pipe and Lyde, Edwyn Ralph, Eau Withington, Pootshill, Wormelow Tump, Clouds, Sunset, The Pludds, Sollers Dilwyn, Laysters Pole, Shortstanding, Stretton Sugwas, Evenjubb, Druggers End, Leinthall Starkes, Tumpy Lakes, Clenchers Mill, The Lonk, The Riddle, Hole in the Wall.

noted for: cider, cattle, Nell Gwynne, Hay, Wye, Didley, Eye, secondhand books

Herefordshire, green and pleasant, is as far as you can go in this direction without stepping into Wales. Back in the 8th century and tired of Celtic incursions, King Offa grabbed a spade and set about the job of detaching Wales from the rest of Britain. According to Asser, writing a hundred years on, Offa was 'a vigorous king, who terrified all the neighbouring kings and provinces around him, and who had a great dyke built from sea to sea between Wales and Mercia.' It was an ambitious scheme, and ultimately one that failed. The canny Welsh found

King Offa

ways over the obstacle long before excavations were completed and the two lands remain firmly joined at the hip. But, as a political statement, it made its mark. George Borrow, writing of local traditions (Wild Wales, 1862), said it 'was customary for the English to cut off the ears of every Welshman who was found to the east of the dyke, and for the Welsh to hang every Englishmen whom they found to the west of it.'

local lingo: Ereford ere, with the odd dash of Welsh
as in: tosticated (drunk) momblement (confusion)

Worcestershire

home to: Cofton Hackett, Cow Honeybourne, Flyford Flavell, Feckenham, Fockbury, Nafford, Grimley, Hagley, North Piddle, Wyre Piddle, Upton Snodsbury, Chaddsley Corbett, Crabbs Cross, Ab Lench, Atch Lench, Croome D'Abitot, Cudley, Tardebigge, Timberhanger, Headless Cross, Thickenappletree, Martin Hussingtree, Grafton Fulford

noted for: Elgar, Malvern Hills, carpets, porcelain, fruit, Lea & Perrins

Worcestershire is still the place to rival Kent for orchards and gardens, apples and pears, plums, cricketers, asparagus and hops. In less peaceful times great battles were fought in this county (Evesham, 1265; Tewkesbury, 1471; Worcester, 1651...). These days the battle is more often with the rising waters of Severn and Avon. Those taking refuge on higher ground. eg Bredon Hill, can be rewarded with a view of 8 to 14 different counties (depending on weather conditions, eyesight, grasp of geography, vividness of imagination and institution of boundary changes ordained by Whitehall).

local lingo: Worcestershire
 as in: dummock (stupid person), scurruck (small bit)

Gloucestershire

home to: Nibley, Wibley, Nup End, North Nibley, Adlestrop, Cambridge, Tiltups End, Dumbleton, Redmarley D'Abitot, Piff's Elm, Leonard Stanley, Snig's End, Duck Hole, Pucklechurch, Harry Stoke, Iron Acton, Cold Ashton, Warmley, Soundwell, Oldbury Naite, Bisley with Lypiatt, Newington Bagpath, Little Herberts, Hucclecote, Humphries End, Paradise
 noted for: cheese rolling, Old Sodbury, flooding, Oldbury tarts

From the Forest of Dean, Glorious Gloucestershire sweeps across the Severn Estuary and up on to the Cotswolds, with its honeypot villages and small towns like Chipping Campden, where the traditional wine bar, deli and village goldsmith still ply their trades. Not far off is Bourton-on-the-Water, which is England's Venice. Only smaller.

Gloucestershire has produced many musicians and composers. Gustav Holst, Herbert Howells, Ivor Gurney and Ralph Vaughan Williams were all born in the county, as was John Stafford Smith, who provided the tune for The Star-Spangled Banner. But so was Jimmy Young.

local lingo: Vorest
 as in: Be you gwain ter pay vor wat you hed?

Glawster, as in: spexso, praps, spose

HOME COUNTIES – BERKSHIRE, BUCKINGHAMSHIRE, HERTFORDSHIRE, MIDDLESEX

Berkshire

home to: Tutts Clump, Trash Green. Stanford Dingley, Ufton Nervet, Halfway, Legoland, Hell Corner, Honey Bottom, Earley Rise, Nobbcrook, Chavey Down, World's End (again)

noted for: rowing, racing, mars bars, swan upping, David Brent

Berkshire's special. Berkshire isn't just Berkshire but the Royal County of Berkshire. What with Windsor, Ascot and Eton, the royal tag comes as no surprise (not to mention Brackley, Tilehurst, Wokingham or Slough). Berkshire is a county of two halves: Posh Berks (going 'dine tine ite to dine') and not-so-posh (going 'dein tein rained the chippie'). Geographically, the county splits at Reading, with leafy Thames off to the east and ridgeway gallops out to the west.

local lingo: Berkshire
    as in: garn away wiv yer, deedy (careful), main deedy (very careful) shucty (shaky), shant (beer), ayt (out), cheeselog (woodlouse)

Buckinghamshire

home to: Knotty Green, Parslow's Hillock, Clanking, Gibraltar, Bledlow cum Saunderton, Hedgerley Dean, Hedgerley Green, Radclive cum Chackmore, Swan Bottom, Stone with Bishopstone and Hartwell

(as with more than a few other counties, Bucks also has its own World's End, California, Egypt, New Zealand etc)

noted for: media folk, Bekonscot nr Beaconsfield (world's oldest model village and inspiration for Noddy & Toytown)

Bucks CC has a coat of arms that features a swan in chains above the motto, *Don't Step Back* (or similar in Latin).

You feel that Buckingham ought to be the county town of Buckinghamshire (as once it was), but it isn't; that honour goes to Aylesbury, while Milton Keynes (part of the ceremonial county of Buckinghamshire) is more than twice the size of both of them.

local lingo: Bucks
as in: jimmy/ Hurdle Bumper (both names for raw sheep's head), quobble (noise a boiling pot makes), rumbustical (boisterous), upstrapalous (obstreperous), odd bodge man, cagmag (tangle), glouty (cross), gooly-bug (ladybird) sotchel/slommuck/ slopput/slotchet (all words for to traipse with slovenly gait)

Eight pints of lager, please, and one small lemonade -

Hertfordshire

home to: The Folly, Much Hadham, Nasty, Smug Oak, Borehamwood, Cold Christmas, Ware

noted for: Nick Faldo, Braughing Sausages

One of Hertfordshire's leading visitor attractions is the Magic Roundabout at Hemel Hempstead. Constructed where seven roads meet, the Moor End roundabout, along with similar in Colchester and Swindon, was one of the first bi-directional roundabouts to be built in Britain. Circling the main roundabout are six mini-roundabouts, enabling traffic to choose whether to venture clockwise or anti- round the main roundabout. The latter hides a small river passing through it; this was the undoing of an articulated lorry that once attempted the direct route. Hemel Hempstead's Modern World Wonder was recently voted 2nd worst roundabout in the UK. Its counterpart in Swindon carried off 1st prize.

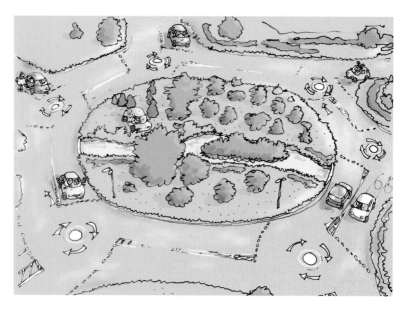

local lingo: Hertfordshire
      as in: edge pooper(sparrow), pimmick (silly fanciful person) wuss, wusser, wusserer, even wusserer

Middlesex
noted for: its demise

Sadly Middlesex has got swallowed up over the years by Greater London, the M25 and all around it. In its fight for survival Middlesex has equipped itself with a vicious looking coat of arms (all blades and notches) and declared May 16th Middlesex Day.

SOUTH EAST – LONDON, KENT, SURREY, SUSSEX

London
The population of London at the last count was 7,185. That's the City of London. Greater London has 7,172,091, leaving 43 million stuck on trains and platforms, trying to get in to work (the population of England is just over 50m). The wider metropolitan area is estimated at 10-14 million.

London, The Smoke, is sometimes described as a series of villages. If so, they haven't half piled up on top of one another. The main division is the N/S divide made by the river; second only to this is the rivalry between East and West (similar to Berlin pre-1989 but without the wall). London also separates into Outer, Inner and Central areas. Almost half (48%) the population of Inner London is aged between 20 – 44 and can be found at any one time with a shopping-bag in Oxford St. (In the rest of England 35% of the population fits into that age-bracket.)

London has the biggest and best of everything, apart from space. Three million trips are made each day on the Tube, which is good news for the makers of under-arm deodorant.

Famous Londoners: Geoffrey Chaucer, Jack the Ripper, Michael Caine, Dot Cotton, Chas 'n Dave

local lingo: Cockney rhyming slang or Rabbit

Kent

home to: Loose, Womenswold, Thong, Easole Street, Bopeep, Thanington Without, Grafty Green, Frindsbury Extra, Old Wives Lees, Monday Boys, Mud Row, Nutts, Knatts Valley, Noahs Ark, Lynsore Bottom, Dumpton, Dully, Cop Street, Plucks Gutter, Pratts Bottom, Snodland, Snargate & Smeeth

noted for: white cliffs, hops, apples, pears, Margate, Dickens, Canterbury

Kent borders E Sussex, Surrey and Greater London. It has a boundary with Essex in the middle of the Thames Estuary, so none of the usual squabbles between gritting lorries from these two counties. Halfway under the Channel, Kent borders with France. That's the point at which your hitherto pleasantly trundling train suddenly goes supersonic, staying gravity-free on mach 5 till somewhere near Perpignan.

Kent saying: the world is divided into five parts: Europe, Asia, Africa, America, Romney Marsh.

local lingo: Kentish

    as in: another when, otherwhere-else, not nohow, because why, before-after, everything-something, dead-alive (dull), diddle-o/amongst the middlins (fair health), wonkly (ill child), weekers (ears), treddles (sheep droppings), snazzums (hiccups), pogger (worrier), progger (mid-morning snack), nabbler (gossip), frigger (fidget), haffy-graffy (almost), high-lows (boots), slummock (slattern), Folkestone girls (heavy rainclouds), umpkey-diddlums (upside-down)

Surrey

home to: Camilla Lacey, Christmas Pie, Donkey Town, Titsey, Friday Street, Ficklesole, Quakers Plat, The Waste, Virginia Water

noted for: trees, millionaires (twice the national average coverage of both)

Surrey County Council administers Surrey from a safe distance beyond the county boundary. Since 1893 the County Council has been based at Kingston upon Thames, which since 1965 has been part of Greater London.

    Also noted for the Surrey Hills: Surrey has golf, mountain biking and a Pipe Band, but is short on chair-lifts and Mountain Rescue teams.

local lingo: Surrey

    as in: on the Bob solly (falling down), bumbly (uneven), hedge fund, derivatives, quantitive easing

Sussex

home to: Cackle Street, Hole Street, Foul Mile, Ball's Cross, Three Leg Cross, Balls Green, Bachelors Bump, Sweethaws, St John Without, Little Whiligh, Harebeating, Lower Dicker, Didling, Mount Noddy, Cocking Causeway, Trotton with Chithurst, Rock Robin, Spotted Cow, Bird in Eye, Great Tott, Glottenham, Grisling Common, Bohemia, Muddleswood, The Dicker, The Bar

noted for: Brighton, Hove, Pond Pudding, stoolball
Sussex motto: We wun't be druv.

East and West Sussex split up in 1189 and have stayed apart since, coming together only to share a Sussex Day (16 June), a county flower (round-headed rampion), an unofficial anthem (Sussex by the Sea) and six martlets, small birds known only to heraldry.

local lingo: Sussex
as in: howsumdever, I bluv, I be dubersome, there was dunnamany people, some one time, generally-always, most-in-general, no one wheres, otherwheres, I goos sarternoon, he be to goo dracly minute, mayhap, I misagree, he suffers from deathness (deaf), hold hard (stop), utchy (cold), blobtit (telltale), beazled (knackered), fornicate (dawdle)

spartacles   slight deathness

SQUATELINGS
(female conversation)

SOUTH WEST – HAMPSHIRE, DORSET, SOMERSET, DEVON. CORNWALL

Hampshire

home to: World's End, Nomansland, Canada, Egypt, Palestine, Vicars Hill, Gins, Romsey Extra, Gobley Hole, Tiptoe, Stratfield Turgis, Ragged Appleshaw, Little Ann, Abbots Ann, Anna Valley, Nately Scures, Golden Pot, Nether Wallop, Up Nately, Faccombe

noted for: Jane Austen, Charles Dickens, Benny Hill, hogs, the Pompey Widdler, Hambledon, West Meon (where Thomas Lord of Lord's lies buried, with Guy Burgess lurking close by), Lymington, Hayling, Hamble . . .

Hampshire is home to sailing and cricket. Once a year the two meet up in mid-Solent, a mile or two off the coast at Calshot. Equinoctial tides in September briefly uncover the Brambles Bank to allow a cricket match of sorts to take place between two local yacht clubs; no shortage of ducks or boundaries, especially towards the end of the game, when tide stops play.

The Pompey Widdler

local lingo: Ampsheer
     as in: Oh, garn on wiv yer, anywhen,
             flittershitters (when something falls apart)

Dorset

home to: Melcombe Bingham, Bingham's Melcombe, Shitterton, Scratchy Bottom, Happy Bottom, Dottery, Droop, Knackers Hole, Lilliput, Nicodemus Knob, Ryme Intrinseca, Toller Fratrum, Tidpit, Folly, Toller Porcorum, Piddletrenthide, Tincleton, Gussage All Saints, Slepe, Up Sydling, Puddletown, Sleeping Green, Melbury Bubb, Iwerne Courtney or Shroton

noted for: knobs, Hardy, Ethelbald, blue vinney

Motto of Dorset CC: *Who's Afear'd* (but no question-mark)

'England's most beautiful county' is the billing on one website (thedorset-page) and it's a claim that plenty of people would go along with, not all of them from Dorset. The claim wears a bit thin around the South East Dorset conurbation also known as Bournemouth. Beyond extends a spectacular coastline, much exploited by writers and home to Old Harry, Portland Bill and the many old fossils of Lyme Bay. Along the way are rarities like Lulworth Cove, Chesil Beach and Golden Cap. Behind is a hinterland of green hills, heathland, stone and thatch, better known as Hardy's Wessex.

local lingo: Daarrset/ Dosset yere

as in: joppety-joppety (nervous jitters), avroze (frozen), tinklebobs (icicles), ruff (roof), chimley, zummat, gert, chockvull, reddick (robin), a-zingen, anywhen, vower (four), geate (gate), volly (follow), grammer (grandma)

CERNE ABBAS, DORSET

That reminds me - did we cancel the milkman?

Somerset

home to: Curryload, Ham, Four Forks, Beer Crocombe, Boozer Pit, Paradise, Lusty, Huish Episcopi, Cricket Malherbie, Clicket (abandoned 1890), Clink, Haselbury Plucknett, Marston Bigot, Mudford Sock, Dead Woman's Bottom, Nempnett Thrubwell, Ubley, Huish Champflower, Vobster, Vole & Oath

noted for: caves, cheese, cider. Levels, iron age forts, Alfred, Arthur, Glastonbury, mud

The motto of Somerset CC is *Sumorsaete Ealle* ('all the people of Somerset and we don't mind how you spell')

Somerset is rich in history and legend, from Arthur and Guinevere to Adge Cutler and the Wurzels. Alfred burnt his cakes here and Acker Bilk in Pensford improved his clarinet technique by losing two front teeth in a school fight and half a finger in a sledging accident. The last pitched battle in England was fought here at Sedgemoor, close to what is now the Westonzoyland Pumping Museum, a must for all addicts of land drainage systems. Weston's Grand Pier, burnt down in 2008 was replaced in 2010 by a '£39m futuristic development' including 4-D cinema, Robocoaster, Freefall, Sidewinder and, er, ghost train. In 2009 the donkeys at Weston were voted top seaside attraction in the annual British Coast awards. Super mares indeed. All right, jennies.

local lingo: Zummerzet
as in: vower, vive, zix, zeben, farty (4,5,6,7,40)
Oi be righ diddlecombe and betwaddled oi be

Bristol

Closely tied up with Somerset and often mistaken for part of it, Bristol is a city that has enjoyed county status in its own right since 1373, apart from a brief spell from 1974 to 1996, when it was Avon instead. Historic port and cultural centre, Bristol has given much to the world, including Bristle, the form of local speech that plays fast and loose with the letter 'l'. This is added to the end of words ending in 'a' or 'o'. Hence bananawl, pataytawl, diarrhoeawl etcl. Not to mention Tescol, Asdawl, Ikeawl, viagrawl . . . You get the general ideal. But, beware funera parlol, minera watawl etcl. Or should that have been genera ideal? Oh, well, back to the drawling-board.

Devon

home to: the English Riviera, Crapstone, Boobery, Bugford, Bogtown, Drizzlecombe, Doddiscombsleigh, Little Potheridge, Red Cow, Splatt, Yondertown, Broadwoodwidger, Black Dog, Holcombe Rogus, Haccombe with Combe, Inner Hope, Higher Hooe, Outer Hope, Pennycomequick, Gabber, George Nympton, Mutterton, Woolfardisworthy, Zeal Monachorum, Woolfardisworthyt'otherone

noted for: red soil, red hair, ruddy cheek, Sir Francis Drake, cream teas, camper vans, Devon Loch, Devon Malcolm, wisht hounds (black dogs with baleful red eyes that roam the moors hunting down sinners and non-believers)

Devon County Council motto is *Auxilio Divino* (Gawd 'elp us)

'England's Best County' is the modest tag that comes up on the website of Visit Devon, official visitor guide to Devon. In fact the line comes from *Country Life*, which surveyed counties in 2003 and again in 2009. Both times top place was awarded to Devon – though the title might reasonably be disputed by the Isle of Wight, which got omitted from the list.

Each county was assessed on a variety of factors, including flood-risk, average property prices (the higher the better), number of entries in Who's Who, tranquillity and number of shotgun licences. As the magazine put it, Devon has 'valleys, deep and wooded, which can only have been formed by a benign providence for one purpose (bang, bang – does that give you a clue?).'

local sports: out-hurling, Devon Wrestling, Hunting of the Earl of Rone

local lingo: Debm, Deben or Demshur
   as in: Ow be nackin vore? You'm lookin praaper thurdle gutted.

Cornwall
home to: St Erme & St Erth, St Tudy & St Teath, St Ewe & St Just in Roseland, Coldwind, Washaway, Sticker, Scarcewater, Stoptide, Splatt, Blue Anchor, Weens, Indian Queens, Goonbell, Goon Gumpas, Great Grogley, Bottoms, Coddles, Fernysplat, Twelveheads, Feock, Flushing, Penhale Jakes, Praze-an-beeble, Perranzabuloe, Polyphant, Merrymeet, Portwrinkle, Penpillick., Wheal Busy, Labour-In-Vain, Sheffield, America, Dobwalls and Trewidland, Afterwashes, Jollys Bottom, Little Beside, Tredrizzickbridge, Trethingey, Trevorrick, Trevarrick, Trungle, Trink. Trelonk, Trelill.

noted for: obby oss, Furry Dance, oggies, hevva cake, stargazy pie, surfers, euchre, Mrs Danvers, the Beast of Bodmin

If the West Country sticks out like a leg on the map, then Cornwall is the foot dangled playfully in the water, with Lizard as heel and Land's End the toe dipped into the ocean. That leaves East Anglia ('allus behind') as bottom and the Thames Gateway as Arsehole of England. It's not a phrase pushed by the Tourist Board of Thurrock.

Cornwall is England's extremity. It's about as far from middle England as you get, except in July and August when Middle England descends on Cornwall for its hols. Cornwall isn't really part of England, more a world of its own: England's largest onshore island. Head west over the Tamar and you soon find things are different, beginning with Kernewek, the language that died out two centuries ago but now is spoken by road-sign makers all over the county.

local lingo: Cornish
as in: Oall Rite Me Hansum? How be knocking fore?
Madderdooee? What ee gakin at? Yer tis.
What doee say? Eee arst arter yew. Ezedun (he said it).
Owaree? Cain telly
Avee? Binundunun. Goynary? (Are you going?). Mentut diddy?
Izza? Areeah!
Mygar!

ISLANDS

Almost all of England's islands are down south; the Isle of Man is not part of England and nor are the Channel Islands, despite being called Les Iles Anglo-Normandes by the French who lay claim to them. Those hanging on in the north form clusters round Furness in the west (Walney, Chapel, Piel and Roa) and Bamburgh in the east (Holy Island and the Farnes). There are 28 Farne Islands (or 40-odd if you count each islet on the map) and 15 when the tide comes in.

England has around 1000 islands, but some of these are blobs in Lake Windermere, some are no longer islands at low tide, some vanish at high tide and some just aren't islands at all. Holy Island (aka Lindisfarne) is one of those like Burgh Island in Devon and St Michel's Mount in Cornwall that can be reached on foot, with an eye on the tide. Getting back is not always so easy. These are respectable islands, even if not so completely surrounded by water as, say, Lundy (or Mundi, as it's known to the French).

The same cannot be said of cheats like Purbeck and Portland. Insular they may be, but fraudulent with it. Some non-isles do have the excuse of a watery past: Isles of Ely, Athelney, Axholme, Wedmore, Oxney ... In Roman times Thanet was separated from Kent by a channel up to two miles across and known as the Wantsum (named after traditional Kentish greeting).

But over the years marshes have been drained and waterways silted up, leaving ex- and semi-islands (Harty and Grain, Oxney and Dogs) high and

dry. For the time being, at least. Sunk Island, once a sandbank in the Humber, is now a village in Yorkshire.

A number of England's islands, like Scolt Head in Norfolk and the Farnes, are inhabited only by birds and by wardens given to much noisy squabbling in the mating season. England's most heavily populated island is Portsea, occupied by Portsmouth, but is it an island? Look out for muddy ditches, not Caribbean-style beaches, along the coastline of Portsea's northern shore. Ditto the many islands of the Essex marshes.

By far the largest island in size is the Isle of Wight, which calls itself The Island and likes to refer to mainland Britain as the North Island. An accident of geography has left the Isle of Wight strangely symmetrical. Straight down the middle runs the River Medina, with East and West Wight spread out each side like wings of a moth. From E & W Cowes the northern shoreline in each direction takes in woodland and creeks before ending in high white cliffs. Just short of each extremity is a harbour at the mouth of a river. Both rivers are called the Yar. And the one in the middle is 'OK-yar'.

The prize for scenic beauty must go to the Isles of Scilly, six of which are inhabited and 140 not. The sixth of these, Gugh, returned a population count of three in the last census. The Island of Samson had ten inhabitants in 1855, but they were evicted to make room for a deer park. The deer did not survive. However, Scilly is the one place in Britain where lives the Lesser White-toothed shrew. The Isles of Scilly Football League has just two clubs, Garrison Gunners and Woolpack Wanderers, both of which have just about had it up to here with playing each other. Note: it's Isles of Scilly, not Scilly Isles, which name belongs to a series of roundabouts on the A307 in Surrey. Anyone heard referring to the place as Scillies or similar gets lashed to a rock till the tide turns. No doubt that's what happened to the author of this prayer which graces a church wall locally:

We pray Thee Lord not that wrecks should happen, but if they do Thou wilt guide them to the Scilly Isles for the benefit of the poor inhabitants.

The English aren't great at welcoming new neighbours on to their patch – not in rural parts anyway, where newcomers and blow-ins are given a 30-year period of probation to work through and are viewed with deep suspicions for the following seventy. One of the ways that family origins are tested is by the pronunciation of local place-names.

PLACES AS SPOKE

PLACES AS SPOKEN

Place-names:
Some lose central component, as in

Hunstanton, Happisburgh, Wymondham, Bicester (Hunston, Hazebruh, Windum, Bister), but Shiplate and Shalfleet do not get shortened thus. Others get known by just their first part: Bovey Tracey, Chapel-en-le-Frith, Sturminster Newton (Bovey, Chapel, Stur), but not Penistone, Scunthorpe or Prickwillow. Aristocrats are some of the worst offenders when it comes to mangling place-names: Cholmondeley ('Chumley'). Beaudesert ('Belser'), Althorp (anyone's guess). But humble settlements can be equally obtuse: Burgh by Sands in Cumbria becomes 'Bruff', while Burgh in Suffolk is 'Berg' (though Blythburgh, also in Suffolk, is 'Blythbruh'). Barugh in S Yorkshire is 'Bark', while Great and Little Barugh in N Yorkshire are 'Barf'.

Now try your hand at these:
Beaulieu, Belvoir, Cowpen, Fowey, Ewell, Frome, Beaminster, Stiffkey, Slaithwaite, Alnwick, Wisbech, Greenwich, Barnoldswick, Prinknash, Puncknowle, Torpenhow, Tintwistle, Leominster, Hoxne, Woolfardisworthy, Beaminster, Furneux Pelham, Seathwaite, Holborn, Marylebone, Mousehole, Gisleham, Shrewsbury, Costessey, Oswaldtwistle, Cley

Score double for any correct answer if of foreign birth (treble if French).

WEST COUNTRY TRADITIONS: MENDING THE NETS

12. Terribly Practical

What are these for?

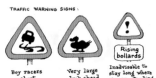

TRAFFIC WARNING SIGNS:

Boy racers about

Very large duck ahead

Rising bollards
Inadvisable to stay long where you are standing

Fire escapes: *for smoking beneath*

Call centres: *for dialling up some of your favourite calming music*

Household Cavalry: *for improving your photos of London*

Roadside red kiosks (pictured): *for widdling in*

Supermarket basket-only checkouts: *for people who can't read*

Citizens Advice Bureau: *will welcome you in and be happy to advise on troubling issues, like whether it's milk in first or milk in after, or whether with scones it's cream on jam or jam on cream*

BUSHEL AND A PECK

The UK went decimal with coinage in 1971. Well, some people did. Those whose schooldays had ended by then generally preferred to stick with what they knew. It seemed simpler:

2 farthings	=	1 halfpenny
8 ha'pence	=	half a groat
3 half-groats	=	1 tanner
4 tanners	=	1 florin
tanner & florin	=	1 half-crown
4 half-crowns	=	10 bob
20 bob	=	1 nicker
nicker & bob	=	1 guinea
25 nicker	=	1 pony

Some useful weights & measures:

1 scruple	=	20 grains
3 scruples	=	1 drachm
1 pennyweight	=	24 grains (Troy)
27.23 grains	=	1 dram (Avoirdupois)
5½ yards	=	1 rod, pole or perch
4 poles	=	1 chain
40 sq chains	=	1 square rood
1 rood	=	40 perches
1.151 miles	=	1 Admiralty knot
1 degree	=	69.121 statute miles

or roughly across the size of Wales

MEDICAL

PARTS OF THE BODY
as taught to medical students from abroad

FIRST AID

What to do in an Emergency

WHAT To Do IN AN EMERGENCY

13. Last Word

BEST IN THE WORLD

Public transport, litter, dogsmuck, languages, coffee ice-cream, caring for the elderly, football, Eurovision Song Contests – there are plenty of things England is lousy at. But there are some in which England can lay some claim to world domination. Try these for starters:

- nutty sleuths (Holmes, Wimsey, Miss Marple, Morse)
- cake (fruit, sponge, Christmas, coffee)
- nudge nudge (Donald McGill, Carry On films, Beryl Cook)
- cottage gardens (roses, wisteria, hollyhocks, lupins)
- puddings with custard (crumble, stodge, treacle tart, mince pie)
- sitcoms (Dad's Army, Fawlty Towers, Porridge, The Office)
- animal charities (Deaf Donkeys, Sick Parrots, Blunt Hedgehogs)
- grand ceremonial (State Opening of Parliament, Strictly, Last Night of the Proms)
- cartoonists (Heath Robinson, Searle, Giles, Thelwell, Larry, Steve Bell)
- drunken youf (Friday night, almost anywhere, also Sat-Sun)
- making lists

Wherever does he get all his ideas from?

14. Revision Pages

Buying A Rail Ticket

Scene: Railway Station, at the Ticket Issuing Facility
Persons: Travel Customer (TC), Travel Card Sales Negotiator (TCSN), queue of 500

TCSN: Hnff?

TC: Phew! Just made it. Fourteen and a half minutes in this queue and my train goes in one min –

TCSN: Hnff!

TC: One standard cheap day return to London, please –

TCSN: *tap, tap, tap, rattle, clunk, sniff, glare*
          Streeble glark buzzfizz fizzbuzz –

TC: Sorry?

TCSN: *adjusting microphone*
          Four thousand three hundred and eighty-two pounds, returning tonight, sir?

TC: Blimey, I could buy Network Rail for half that, couldn't I?

TCSN: Or four pound eighty if you'd asked a month ago.

TC: What about with this travel card?

TCSN: Wozzat?

TC: Over 30s Corridor Club SupaSaver Bonus Card

TCSN: Ninety-eight pounds thirty plus free forehead sticker. Do you want Anytime or Offpeak, Ranger or Rover, multi-modal or exclusive?

TC: Or this one, Patio Decking Owners' Club Price Squeezer Citirail Budget Cool Travel Pass?

TCSN: Sixteen pounds forty why didn't you say so before?

TC: I'll have it –

TCSN: That is on the West Line route, changing at Fawley, Crawley, Horley, Penge –

TC: Jus' gimme –

TCSN: With travel valid only between the hours of 0200–0600, that's three pounds sixty change –

TC: That's my train gone now –

TCSN: Not with that ticket it ain't. Some people just don't get it, do they? Next –

CONVERSATION PRACTICE (2)

On The Telephone

Persons: Telesales caller (T), Ronald F, householder (R)

T: dring dring . . . dring dri-

R: Hello.. hello . . . hell-

T: . . . .

R: 429873 hello . . .

T: . . . clickzonkgubblefizz . . . Hi, Ron –

R: Hello..

T: This is zonkgubblewhirr my name's fizzgubble this is just a courtesy call to

R: But I don't want any –

T: First I must warn you that, for purposes of training, this call may be recorded –

R: I said I didn't want –

T: Hold it, Ron, I need first to check a few details for purposes of security. Your name is Ron –

R: No, it's Fleasmould. Mr. And it's Ronald.

T: Ok, Ron. Now date of birth?

R: Hang about, I'm not telling you that. How do I know who you are anyway? You could be stealing my identity. Or are you the feller opposite with the binoculars behind the curtains?

T: . . . fuzzbugglezonkstatutory requirement and without it I'm not able to unsubscribe you from our Finance Friendship Line. All banks have to do this.

R: All right, all right, 5.3.42.

T: That's 0-5, 0-3, er 19-42?

R: Tsk.

T: And last two letters of mother's maiden name?

R: HT.

T: Sorry?

R: HT.

T: That's not what we have here.

R: Are you telling me I can't even spell my own middle name?

T: No, no, of course not, but we have something different onscreen here. Tell me, Ron, do you have issues with dyslexia in your family?

R: I most certainly do not and if you are not capable of spelling the name I gave you – are you in India?

T: I'm sorry, but if you wish to change your name or other details, you need to visit your bank, taking passport, birth certificate, gender re-assignment papers and two recent utility bills –

R: For f***'s sake –

T: I have to warn you that aggressive or abusive language will not be tolerated on this courtesy line and all details will automatically be passed on to the police . . .
Now, Ron . . . Hello? Hello, Ron? Ron? Ok, I'll call back later.

FREQUENTLY ASKED QUESTIONS

Who? Where? Why? Why not?

ENGLISH CITIZENSHIP TEST

Practice Papers

Tick one answer for each question –

Section One: General Knowledge

1. Marmite is used to –
   blacken grates
   polish shoes
   smear on chest and lip in case of heavy cold
   deter ants

2. Inside the costume of Sooty was the young –
   Ronnie Corbett
   Daniel Corbett
   Olga Korbut
   Albert Steptoe

3. Marmalade is made from –
   carrots
   swede
   goldfish
   kittens

4. Odd one out –
   Hezza
   Prezza
   Gazza
   Wozza

5. in the 14th over of the 3rd Test v Borneo in 1948, JB Phillipps scored –
   6 runs
   7 runs
   8 runs
   9 runs

6. Which of the following has not been a regular member of the panel of Gardeners' Question Time?
   Roy Boulting
   Daphne Mildew
   Blossom Wilt
   Hermione Mangold

7. The quickest way to get from Leeds to Liverpool is by –
   M 621 – M 62 – roadworks – diversion – back on to M 62 – M 61 –
   M 6 – M 58 – M 57 – M 62
   canal
   tram
   plane from Gatwick

8. Peter goes out and buys two gobstoppers (at a ha'penny each), one tin of dubbin (at one and nine) and a small detached house (at seven and six). How much change does he have left from his ten-bob note?
   one florin

one fathom
two firkins
five farthings

Section Two: Social Customs

1. When pouring tea, which should land first in the cup?
    sugar lump
    milk
    tea
    Worcester sauce
    ginger nut biscuit

2. At a mini-roundabout drivers should give way to:
    everything
    nothing
    4 × 4s
    17 yr olds with big sound systems

3. Royalty should be addressed as:
    Mam
    Marm
    Mom
    Mum
    Mayhem
    Majestic

4. In England it is polite to curtsey to:
   traffic-wardens
   choirboys
   estate agents
   chestnut trees
   all of the above, but not on Thursdays

5. Pronounce correctly:
   i) Keighley, Haughley, Rougham, Brougham, Sproughton, Claughton, Loughborough, Pettaugh, Ellough, Clough, Oughtershaw, Slough, Boughton Aluph, Humshaugh, Rough Common
   ii) Leigh (in Surrey), Leigh (in Kent), Leigh (Lancs)
   iii) the three trap districts of Milton Keynes: Loughton, Broughton, Woughton

6. Place in order of precedence:
   Ashley Cole
   Lily Cole
   Cheryl Cole
   Ole King Cole

Index